Ghost Man
Reflections on Evolution, Love, and Loss

Thomas Simmons

© 2001 by Thomas Simmons. All rights reserved.

No part of this book may be reproduced, stored in a retrieval system, or transmitted by any means, electronic, mechanical, photocopying, recording, or otherwise, without written permission from the author.

ISBN: 0-7596-6428-5

This book is printed on acid free paper.

1stBooks - rev. 10/23/01

The following poems quoted in this manuscript are used by permission of the authors, who have retained copyright:

"The Garden" by Robert Pinsky, from *History of My Heart* (New York: Ecco Press, 1984); "Trout Watching" by Kenneth Fields, from *Smoke* (Duluth, Minnesota: Knife River Press, 1975); "To You, Seated Near a Lamp" by Diane Middlebrook, from *Sequoia: Twentieth-Anniversary Issue, Poetry 1956-1976*, ed. Michael J. Smith and Dana Gioia (Stanford, 1976); "To the Unseeable Animal" by Wendell Berry, from *Collected Poems* (Berkeley: North Point Press, 1984); and "In the Park" by Maxine Kumin, from *Nurture: Poems* (New York: Penguin, 1989).

Also by Thomas Simmons

Nonfiction

The Unseen Shore: Memories of a Christian Science Childhood

A Season in the Air: One Man's Adventures in Flying

Literary Criticism

Erotic Reckonings: Mastery and Apprenticeship in the Work of Poets and Lovers

For Thomas Elijah

who may one day ask the same questions

Contents

Acknowledgments xi

Prologue xv

Part I: Ghost Man 1
    Crow Pass, 1992 3
    Coda 15
    The Garden 18
    Shotgun 22
    Backbone 27
    Love 32
    Ghost Man 40

Part II: Rifleman 47
    Rifleman 49
    The Woman Who Married a Bear 70
    Primates 83
    Hasidim: A Seventeen-Year Postscript 101

Epilogue 107

Notes 137

Acknowledgments

Like many books, though perhaps fewer than in the past, this book required a considerable number of years of reading, traveling, living and dying, writing, and revising. Early influences for which I am still profoundly grateful came from the all too rare confluence of compassion and brilliance at MIT. Alan Lightman, distinguished physicist and novelist and head of the Program in Writing and Humanistic Studies during my last year at MIT, helped create a zone of safety when I most needed it. Dr. Eric Chivian, member of Physicians for Social Responsibility and Nobel Peace Prize winner, did the same. Samuel Jay Keyser, esteemed linguist and associate provost, and Dan Rothman, professor of Earth, Atmospheric, and Planetary Studies, were consistent inspirations. One other compatriot at MIT was more essential than she could possibly know.

In the years since my departure from that crucible, I was fortunate to have the assistance of two deans—Judith Aiken and Linda Maxson—of the College of Liberal Arts at the University of Iowa. Their willingness to provide two semester leaves for me—one in 1995 and one in 2001—enabled me to prepare this book for publication in a way that might otherwise have been impossible. I would also like to thank two English department chairs—Ed Folsom and Brooks Landon—for providing departmental support for these leaves. Their quiet encouragement made the entire project go forward. I am grateful as well to Professor Emeritus Carl Klaus for providing a thoughtful reading of an earlier version of the manuscript, and to Professor Laura Rigal for offering an encouraging critique of the epilogue. A highly entertained response to part of the epilogue from Professor Kevin Kopelson also deserves acknowledgment.

Several graduate students also inquired about the project as it grew, and their readings of part or all of the manuscript proved especially helpful. Having pondered the first two sections of an earlier draft of the manuscript, Corrine Richardson Madden referred me to the poetry of Stephen Dobyns, and particularly to the poem "Querencia," which serves as the epigraph to the current epilogue. Chelsea Snow Cain, a student in the masters program in journalism, author of the memoir *Dharma Girl: A Road Trip across the American Generations*, and editor of the anthology *Wild Child: Girlhoods in the Counterculture*, offered a thoughtful reading of this book when I most needed it. Byron Wickstrom Murphy, a student in the MFA program in nonfiction but also a teaching assistant in biology, found this material sufficiently interesting that he directed me to a wealth of additional reading in psychology, neurology, and biology.

As I write these acknowledgments, six years after the first draft of this book came into being and a few weeks after its final revision, I realize how many other debts are explicit and implicit in this book—some repayable, others not. Henrietta Buckmaster, a former editor of the "Home Forum" of the *Christian Science Monitor*, appears in this book at the beginning of the essay "Primates"; I realize now that it is possible to read that portrait somewhat critically, particularly given my other writings on the Christian Science religion. In fact, no reading could be more inappropriate. Henrietta Buckmaster was one of the miraculous people I have met in my life, at once the most fierce and most compassionate, a divine emissary whose polio was, in the end, only a minor inconvenience. She worked at the *Monitor* during its heyday, before its near-destruction in the late 1980's (the full story of this, as well as the full story of the religion itself, can be found in Caroline Fraser's *God's Perfect Child: Living and Dying in the Christian Science Church*). I was privileged to serve as an intern to her, and to several other editors: Earl Foell, Editor-in-Chief; David Anable, International Editor; David Winder, Deputy International Editor; and Lucille DeView, Intern Editor and reporter without peer.

Those who have read two of my earlier books—*The Unseen Shore: Memories of a Christian Science Childhood* and *A Season in the Air: One Man's Adventures in Flying*—may assume that my lifelong encounters with Christian Science have been uniformly devastating, but this is not entirely true. My summer as an intern at the *Christian Science Monitor* in 1979 was the best work experience of my life (a rather melancholy admission in the year 2001). The intellectual acumen, worldly experience, and intuitive generosity of the editors, reporters, and staff of that newspaper have never been equaled in any university in which I have studied or served as a professor. Historians may disagree somewhat on what damaged that newspaper and dispersed much of its talent almost 15 years ago, but those of us who worked there remember what happened, know who was responsible, lament the loss, and admire the recent work of incipient restoration. We also remember the distinction of the achievement, the immense pleasure of the work, the deep comaraderie, the lasting legacy. Despite my fierce disagreements both with the theology of Christian Science and with its application to children and young adults, I can only honor here my time and my colleagues at the *Christian Science Monitor*.

I remain equally indebted to several professors who in the late 1970's taught at Stanford University—Kenneth Fields and Diane Middlebrook, who continue at Stanford, and N. Scott Momaday, now a chaired professor at the University of Arizona. Each of these three teachers confirmed something about the relationship of literature and intuitive truth in my life. For each of them at that time, literature was an avenue to intuitive truth, and because this truth existed it was in some way impervious to the extremely fad-conscious swings of literary and cultural theory. Though this point of view may seem to many readers thoroughly outmoded now, and though at least one of these professors has moved quite some theoretical and critical distance from that earlier stance, I could at the time have had no greater consolation for the loss of my religion than the teaching of these three professors. I am also especially grateful to Professor Emeritus Ronald Rebholz of Stanford, whose essential kindness, critical keenness, and articulate outspokenness became for me a model of excellence (and a model of self-defense) in the often hostile and unseemly world of the university.

My dear friend Michael Ramsey-Perez, a former graduate student at Stanford and a poet whose life's fortunes spun into a whirlwind somewhat similar to my own, nevertheless was kind enough to offer me a room in his beautiful home in Palo Alto, California in the fall of 1995, when I was trying to bring the first draft of this book together in the midst of unprecedented upheaval. My only regret is that, whatever despair I confronted at that time, Michael himself was to undergo shortly afterwards in a somewhat different context; if I had known how to prevent that descent, I would have done so. My gratitude for Michael's generosity is endless.

Some of this book concerns my relationship with my ex-wife Lesley Wright, whom I first met when I was a junior in high school and to whom I was married for 17 years. It may be uncommon to acknowledge one's debt to a woman with whom one has shared perhaps the ultimate severance of divorce, yet despite our differences we had unities that should not go unnoticed; among these are forgiveness for the trial by fire that we inadvertently created for each other. Our children, Nathaniel and Georgia, grow more wonderful each day, and this in itself is a testament to her skill and grace as a human being. However much our paths have diverged, my life would have been immeasurably less worth living without her.

However it may seem to readers, this book is distinctive in part because its publishing history is both odd and, I suspect, increasingly common. The first half of the book, and particularly the first essay, appear to be straightforward autobiographical meditation; the second half of the book tends more militantly toward a mix of autobiography and intellectual reflection. This mix doomed the book at every press it visited. Five trade New York publishers rejected it, after which it lost the attention of its New York agent; one trade publisher in Boston rejected it, after which its Boston agent made several kind editorial suggestions that, for various reasons, proved unworkable; and an even dozen university presses also rejected it, including the University of Washington Press, the University of Georgia Press, the University of Oklahoma Press, the University of Nebraska Press, the University Press of New England, the University of Illinois Press, Indiana University Press, and even the press closest to home, the University of Iowa Press. Though the specific reasons for these eighteen rejections differed slightly, the main reason—repeated so often that it could almost serve as a refrain—was that the book was too much of a "hybrid": too intellectual for the "average" reader, it was also too mainstream (or perhaps too "average") for the intellectual reader. It lacked sufficient drama, gossip, or dirt to be hot autobiographical material; it lacked sufficient notes, appendices, and disciplinary loyalty to be a work of scholarship. In the end, it was simply an orphan, or something illegitimate whose pedigree was questionable enough to warrant discreet confinement to a desk drawer.

This I refused to believe. After nearly a decade of writing and revision, I am willing to admit that I may be wrong—this book may, in fact, be too eccentric to be a book—but I am not yet convinced that I am wrong. Although, in retrospect, I might have taken some of these earlier essays in a somewhat different direction, I can find no reason to apologize for this book, nor any reason to hide it. I am grateful to Paul Burt, Associate Director of Author Services at 1stBooks Library in Bloomington, Indiana, and to his staff, for their grace and intelligence on behalf of this book. At the same time, I would like to thank especially the one person who urged me to find a new avenue for the publication of *Ghost Man*. Elizabeth Collins, an MFA student at the University of Iowa, gently drummed back into my head the hope that every editor and agent with whom I corresponded had gently annihilated. To the extent that this book merits serious public attention, I must thank Elizabeth for making it so. To the extent that this book manifests my own flaws and my own ignorance as a writer and as a human being, I must take full responsibility.

—Tom Simmons
Grinnell, Iowa
October 2001

Prologue

Nine years ago, after I had left MIT for the University of Iowa, after I had nearly gotten divorced but had, at the last minute, reunited with my wife, and after I had concluded provisionally that human love made no sense, I began writing this book. One thing I seemed to be good at was writing, or rather writing and publishing (the essential requirement of the university professor, although in all these years no one that I know of has really demonstrated a clear relationship between intelligence and publication). Over the previous decade or so I had published over 100 articles, and between 1990 and 1992 I published or acquired contracts for three books. These books together were one of two central pleasures in my life, the other being fatherhood: at least, I thought, I could quickly pull together a reasonable book and take good care of my kids. Thus I sat down, in December 1992, to begin this book, a project I thought might consume perhaps a year or at most a year and a half. Little did I know.

The two ideas most on my mind were the theory of love as a "post-evolutionary" force, undetermined by genetics and perhaps more dangerous than most things that *could* be genetically determined; and the idea that love was somehow bound up with a "home range," a right place for any specific human to live and grow, and that—in the absence of this home range—a human might suffer as severely as, say, a bear might suffer. Darwin, of course, talked to some extent about the first of these ideas in *The Descent of Man*, but I wanted to explore them with more specific examples of consequence, of loss. The curiosity about home ranges evolved in part from a trip to Alaska I took in 1992, but in part for earlier reasons.

These ideas were especially compelling to me because, having moved from northern California to a suburb of Boston in July 1988, I found myself more off-balance than I could remember being for many years. Nothing in my life compared to the foreignness of the Belmont-Cambridge line in Massachusetts, where my wife and two-year-old son and I came to live in the middle flat of a narrow, drab "triple-decker" in a narrow, drab, run-down neighborhood of flats and condominiums (all of which sold then for well above $100,000, well above our range). We came to this from a place where we could walk out of our apartment (in Palo Alto, California) and backpack for two or three days along a series of trails out of town and up into the Pacific coastal range all the way to the Pacific Ocean, a few miles north of Santa Cruz. We came from a place where, despite the amoral development of Silicon Valley, earth and terrain and foliage and trees and sky and ocean and wilderness remained essential.

My wife and I took our identities from these places. She seemed to have what animal biologists would call a "home range" from about 20 miles north of

Yosemite to about 40 miles south of Kings Canyon; I had a home range along the northern coast of California between Bolinas and Rockport. Actually, an animal biologist—someone like R. Edward Grumbine or Jon Almack—would surely get edgy about this use of "home range," and for good reasons, but the idea that my wife and I became more clearly who we were in these places (and the fact that these places were actually rather widely separated) meant something so important to us that we seemed not to realize what we had lost until, waking up one morning in 95% humidity and 90-degree weather in an un-air-conditioned flat that cost us more than half my MIT salary to rent, we looked at each other with the simple horror of creatures who have no idea where they are or what they have done.

Four years straight from Hieronymus Bosch passed, as I struggled with my job at MIT and as we struggled as a family, mostly on one relatively small income, with first one and then two children. There were a few good days, many bad ones. Over time, I realized that I could not feel what I had once called "love"; it no longer seemed to be within me. There was a terrible emptiness, as if weariness could be shaped into a mine shaft and one's soul could drop down into it, farther and farther and slower and slower, the bottom never to be reached. And so I began to think what at the time seemed like strange thoughts.

I began to think that love does *not* appear necessary for the survival of the species; on the contrary, the presence of passionate love, and the way it binds people to each other for potentially arbitrary reasons and then blows them apart, seemed to me terribly destructive. Lower orders of animals, such as dogs or cats, seemed to me, in their copulations and manifestations of devotion and distance, to be much better off. I began, in my spare time, to read about bears, which interested me both in themselves and in the ways they occupied American Indian story telling, particularly Kiowa storytelling (which, because of my studies many years before with N. Scott Momaday at Stanford, was the storytelling I knew best). Bears, it seemed to me, knew modes of behavior and modes of strength that humans could only envy. I also began to encounter my first stories of American Indian shamanism, which interested me greatly as an alternative to the Christian Science childhood I had had. The power of animals in this spiritually-immanent performance had a reality that the kinds of prayers I had encountered as a child had always lacked.

By the summer of 1991, when my first book (about Christian Science) had appeared and (because Boston is the home of the Christian Science Mother Church) I faced a barrage of media interviews and criticism, I had begun to regret my humanity itself: humans seemed truly to me to be an aberration on the planet. Only my encounters with transcriptions of American Indian oral literature kept me sanguine enough to continue with my life—or, rather, only those encounters and my emerging love of flying, which took me off the earth in a way that made human ingenuity seem hopeful and freeing. I began to have dreams, at about that time, of flying, naked, across wide expanses of earth, around thick branches of trees, landing softly, and taking off once more; they were, I learned later, a type of initiatory shamanic dream, but at the time they were simply marvelous. I wanted never to wake up. But always there was another morning, another variation of Bostonian bleakness, another obligation at MIT, another loss or failure or surprising reversal of some kind or another.

Once I left MIT in June 1992—having burned a swath of loss so wide that I could barely see the horizon beyond the smoke—I felt that I knew three things: I was lost; it was in the nature of the human experience to be, repeatedly, lost; and I did not understand why this should be. I was stubborn. If love *were* post-evolutionary, at once a promise and a danger to the species, then how did that promise or danger truly manifest itself? Was it possible that love was connected to the human investment in storytelling? If so, was it possible that something more reliable than what we usually called "love" existed at, say, a pre-linguistic or post-linguistic level of consciousness? *Was* there such a thing as a level of conscious awareness that preceded language (as Henri Bergson suggested early in the previous century and as numerous linguists and cognitive scientists have averred since then)? *Was* there such a thing as a post-linguistic level of consciousness, in which a body of feeling and experience emerged from the horror or the triumph of story and then surpassed it, so that story-telling was no longer necessary? And what did any of this have to do with the human quest—or any species' quest—for a home range, for a place of wide refuge?

These seemed (perhaps typically, given my background) like intellectual questions to me, and I thought—in December 1992—that I could thus approach this book as if it were "just another book," another way to demonstrate my abilities as a writer and my employability as a professor, as if what mattered most were (in Jean Baudrillard's phrase) my ability to maintain the "code of production" mandated in my corner of the culture. I had no idea, nine years ago, how this book would open the door on even wider terrors and losses—how it would finally project the divorce and desolation I had both wanted and sought to avoid—and how it would confront me finally with a view of my humanity that did not really look like anything I had seen before. Much humbling would have to occur before any sense could emerge, and that humbling, which took the better part of a decade, was—as humbling tends to be—unpredictable, seemingly undesirable, and finally ineradicable.

What follows, then, are essays linked by time, place, and theme, written as if they were rents in the veils across increasingly desolate places, and yet generally leading nowhere near the intended destination. The ghost man who writes them has, perhaps, the advantage of knowing his ghostliness, but in the end even he is surprised: there is something solid behind the ghost, and his most secret yearnings, after all. It is reasonable to wonder, however, whether the book was worth the journey. In the end, this journey, it seems, was—as must be true for most people, the writers and the storytellers and the silent—worth only the journey itself: the product, perhaps, was irrelevant. And yet: here is that product, that book, that work of a ghost man who is also, at least, a man.

PART I

Ghost Man

Thomas Simmons

Crow Pass, 1992

There had been two deaths by mauling in southern Alaska within the month, and on this mid-August afternoon I was the only solitary hiker on the Crow Pass trail. Everyone else traveled in pairs or groups, and carried large-bore pistols or rifles. The leader of the largest group I passed—six or seven backpackers—had a hunting pistol in his belt, pirate-style, and gave me an uncomprehending look as I stumbled by him near the A-frame shelter at the pass. I glanced back at him once as I gained a few yards: he stared in disgust, theatrically, as if to point out to his companions how stupid some people could be. It was the Chugach National Forest, Alaska, after all, not some county park in the lower 48. I had a backpack, tent, sleeping bag, cook kit, Swiss Army knife, map, compass, food. No gun, no hunting knife, not even a hiking stick.

I'd read the bear reports before coming up here. But a sudden freezing spell or snow storm seemed more likely to me in this latitude than a bear sighting, and I'd filled my pack with extra clothes instead of a gun. I'd never owned a gun anyway, didn't know how to shoot one, and didn't have the money to buy one. It made more sense to me to take a chance on death by mauling than by freezing.

Last winter, when for various reasons my life was falling apart, I suddenly realized that I would rather die than live a certain kind of life. I said this to myself one day in the empty, newly-painted room of an apartment I had rented for myself after separating from my wife. I had no idea what I was doing, but I knew that life for me could not continue the way it had always been. The thought was as peaceful and as chilling as the winter air flooding through the open window of the room.

But I did not want to die. I wanted to go on living. I wanted to live something better—not less responsible or less serious, but *better*, harder, more delicious, more full of love. I did not know how. But I felt then, at least, that if at some point I came to believe my life was hopeless I could choose between living and dying. It was not a choice I had ever offered myself before. Having it in mind made living possible.

It did not, however, make living better, at least by itself, because so much of what I was living had become tangled in loss. I had lost my wife; I had lost someone else very precious to me, someone I imagined to be intimately in my future; and I had lost a former understanding of myself, a vision of stability and productivity. I had almost nothing to replace these losses, only a dim vision of survival. Now, months later, the possibility of dying traveled lightly with me, as it did when I first made the choice, as it would—I hoped—in any risky situation in the future. "Who are you, and what do you love?" I pared my questions down to those two, and in the silence of my inability to answer I hoped I was in the hands of grace.

It was already late afternoon, and although I could have gone several hours farther in the sub-Arctic light, I decided to make camp about 500 feet above the trail, across from Raven glacier. The glacier itself, an eighth of a mile wide and a quarter-mile or so long, sloped down into the valley below me; its indifferent blueness was a kind I had never seen before, as if Tahitian water had been turned in a flash to ice. Tired from the climb to this spot, and short on water, I scrambled over heavy scree to catch some of the glacial run-off. At the edge of the glacier I stood on an unsteady slope of small slabs of rock, peering up into crevasses that looked as if they might freeze me instantly. The other hikers had all passed by; there was no one else around.

What was the chance, I wondered, of meeting a bear here? For safety's sake, back in camp, I moved my cook kit several hundred feet away from the tent, piling rocks on and around my bag of food because there were no trees in which to hang it. I began to get a sense, finally, of being alone. Being alone with one's thoughts when one thinks too much can be a bad thing, and mealtimes in the mountains are moments of truth for me. One terrifying thought, one recollection of a family tragedy or an ugly newspaper headline or something else that suggests the savagery of human beings, and my mind can quickly go bad, like an electronic device spiked in a power surge. Sitting near the tiny, gasoline-powered stove, I listened to the dim staccato sputtering of its flame until the sound vanished. When I looked, I could see the steam rising from the boiling water, but could hear only a wide sound that seemed like the sound of the wind if it were frozen. I heard it all around me, but inside me too, so that it was impossible to tell whether anything but me was making it. I thought I was hearing the glacier, but when I glanced over at it, the sound went away. And I remembered a movie, and my mind went bad.

I had gone to a friend's birthday party in Avalon, New Jersey when I was nine or ten. For a special treat we were driving over to the next town to see a new western about a hunt for a rampaging grizzly. It was a beautiful summer day, I was happy, and my friend and I kidded each other and flung each other around without seat belts in the back of his father's Pontiac LeMans convertible. In the darkened theatre, I waited with delight.

But then I saw the entire ranch wiped out, calves and cows lying on their sides, bleeding, guts protruding, and I felt nauseated and wanted to get out. There was no way out; there was only the movie. My friend was spellbound. I could make out the trace of his father's smile in the darkness. The bear was enormous, unvanquished until the end when the hero-father of the family, even as he was being savagely mauled, fired the fatal shot. I saw the father slouched, panting, as his son ran to him; his torso was bloodied, but he looked OK, like a wounded hero. Then he turned his head to face the boy, and half of it was simply gone. My body froze in the theatre; I could not breathe. The father, who tried to comfort his son, would die.

I try to distract myself from these memories, but cannot. The blood I see is my own, and in that fatal darkness all distinctions meld: I am the father and the boy and the bear as well, but not the bear in any way I know, and as I stand up and stretch and walk back to the tent to calm myself the sight of the bear in my child's memory leaps forward with a sound like a roar, like running water or a glacier slowly crushing the stone beneath it, and I leap suddenly, gently off a bluff near my tent down the trail below, hoping in the brief fall to clear my mind of the fear. It works: I touch down, turn back to see the steam from my camp stove, and hear only the silence again.

Thought is alienation from life, but not all thought—not the thought that makes poems or feeds the hungry or heals the heart. I carry with me a huge dross of unknowing—visions of who I might be or am too afraid to be, what I might do or have no skill to do, old hatreds and wishes for revenge, murderous imaginings, fears of victimhood. And these are all me, but they are not me: they inhabit my life like relatives bent on chaos. I feed them, take care of them, nurture them, run from them, because I am intimately related to them. But as I come to suspect them for the harm they cause, I wonder if I can ever journey far enough and fast enough to outrun them. Is that possible? Or will I just circle around to meet them again?

The stew I'm cooking is almost done; I spoon it out of the pot into a Sierra cup I picked up in Anchorage a couple of days ago. It's strange how all my equipment for this trip is thrown together. Old beloved things, like my original Sierra cup from years ago, got lost when I moved out, and yet I have the family stove, and my sleeping bag, perhaps my most prized possession of all, though I bought it only ten months ago to keep me company when it was clear I would be alone for a time. Even this trip seems thrown together, a sudden decision after months or years of fantasy. I'm not quite sure why I'm here; as with so many old plans, their roots bound in a child's desires and frustrations, this plan has come to look very different from what I intended. And yet, finally, I have come here.

A noise at my back makes me turn, not suddenly but with a smoothness that surprises me. Two hunters, armed with high-powered rifles and scopes, nod as they pass behind me on the way up the ridge. I remember catching sight of them on the trail a couple of hours earlier. They may be father and son—not quite lookalikes, but with a trace of kinship in the set of the eyes, the motion of the arm opposite the rifle as they hike. They look slightly embarrassed, as if they had intruded on my wide-open privacy.

"Seen anything up here?" the younger one asks.

"No bear, if that's what you're looking for."

"Oh, we're looking for most anything," says the older one with a smile that doesn't quite suit his face. "Sheep, bear—ain't seen nothin' so far."

"We thought you'd be clear down the valley by now," says the other.

We've talked too long. They're already moving up the ridge. "Take it easy," one of them yells, and they're out of my life.

A slow mist is moving up the valley, but if I look straight up I can still see blue sky, and contrails of jets on the way to Europe or Japan—long threads turning into clouds and slowly disappearing. So much traveling going on, I think idly, wondering what I would be doing now if I'd stayed home in Iowa. It's as if a lead door drops down on my imagination: I can't see home at all. I can see my children, and my wife Lesley, now gathered for a vacation in California with her relatives, and I can see one or two other people I love and a random assortment of other things and places—but not home.

There is an intense quiet about this place, now that evening is settling in, the other hikers and hunters making camp a mile or two miles or more from here, the sounds of people giving way to wind over rock. Because I think too much, I want to make something of this quiet, to make great meaning from it or to show myself how it might direct my life; I want it to be part of a myth that people turn over and over and unravel for meaning. But it's just quiet. The simplicity of it defeats my purpose, and as I look out over the deep crevasses of Raven glacier, I go back, not to myth, but to a well-worn story I tell myself, one that may have no ending.

II

She said: "What is it you want?"
I said: "I want you to be free."
She looked away. The air from her lips shaped itself into a tuneless disgust.

It was near midnight, mid-November 1991, in Boston. We were drinking whatever was most available in a café on Charles Street, surrounded by students and couples on weekend vacations. The din was enormous, increasing our privacy; our thunder spread out through the room without anyone noticing.

I looked at this beautiful woman, thinking how sad and tired she looked, how sad and tired I had looked that evening in the mirror as I shaved. It was impossible to track the ways things had gone from roads to paths to wasteland; we were lost. A few months ago, I had found myself through her; a light that had been dimming for years came brightly back, and I could see again what was lovely and possible in the world. It was she who invited my imagination to take old risks. And it seemed that I was able to do the same for her.

How had I lived before meeting her? I had done conventional things, though not always in conventional ways. I had gone to graduate school, had written an odd dissertation on American poetry, had gotten a job as an assistant professor at MIT. I had felt the noose of competition tighten at every step, and I had assented to breathing a little less deeply every time so that I might continue, so that I might earn a certain professional distinction and earn a living for myself and Lesley, also a graduate student with a limited fellowship, and our two children.

Lesley and I had married more than a decade earlier, and had been together even longer than that. If we had come from a fairy tale, it would have been one in which two children, paired happily but irrevocably separated by some wicked creature, recombined through a miraculous spell in adulthood. Our affinities, when we found each other in high school, were very strong. At our best moments we felt a kind of grace following us, putting us at ease with each other when many of our friends were morose, frightened, or angry with their lovers. Our differences were equally strong. There were subjects we could not easily discuss, intimate matters of religion and neurosis, and moments when we felt, with each other, as alone as we had ever felt in our lives. But learning aloneness was part of the human condition, and besides, when we clicked we felt an old kinship come to life.

Perhaps it was too old a kinship; perhaps we took it too much for granted; or perhaps it was more fragile than we had ever thought. When it began to fade, it did so with such a gradual sullenness that we almost did not notice. When we did, finally, notice, locked so fiercely into our deadening routines and debts in the summer of 1991, we felt as if we had been dropped into the end of one of Henry James' later novels. The practical problems had become habitually real: I would try to explain that we could not live on one income when we were running $1,000-a-month deficits, that we could not afford $700 a month for daycare if she was not actually going to use that time to finish her dissertation; she would argue with ferocious contempt that I was trying to undermine her career; I would take on additional work, extra teaching, and come home even more exhausted, more angry; she would refuse to search for a job; I would apply for other jobs, and get offers, but they all paid even less than what I made at MIT. Lost dollars and intransigence seemed to make our skeletons shine through our skin in the thin evening light of our flat. Aware that something had gone terribly awry, we could not describe what had happened to us except in stunted, unfinished dialogues. On the surface all seemed well. Our relatives were pleased with us. Ours was a classic behavior, and thus we were not losing; we were winning.

But my heart was failing. The chest pains I came home with in the evenings turned out to be more psychosomatic than anything else, but their metaphor was unignorable. I could not continue on the path I had chosen. Something essential within me was dying. I learned to fly airplanes as a way of searching for what was dying and trying to save it; in doing so I opened a door on some very old fantasies—hopes for life that had nothing to do with universities, or with any conventional jobs. I recalled my old desire to make a living as a bush pilot, and I remembered my love of places—how I wanted, not so much to do something, but to be somewhere. Usually the somewhere was relatively remote—the northern Sonoma coast in California, the coast of Oregon, the Olympic peninsula, Denali.

The woman who sat across from me had written, in a class I had taught some months before, about places I loved: she knew them well. After the last class—when I had brought her John McPhee's book on Alaska, and she had brought me a luminously-glazed pot she had made, a "failure" that had been waiting on her shelf for the right occasion—we began to talk about the Olympic peninsula, and the work she'd done there for the Forest Service, and the places we'd live if we could.

"Do you sometimes love places more than people?" I asked suddenly. She looked surprised. "I mean, I've sometimes asked friends if they have any places that are more important to them than people, or most people. They just look at me like I'm a little crazy."

She smiled. "No one's ever asked me that before."

A few weeks later, with a sheaf of world aeronautical charts of Alaska in my bag, I canceled my afternoon office hours and went out into the cool September sun to meet this new soulmate. On a grassy spot by the Charles River, we spread the charts out, one by one, until all of Alaska lay before us. As we knelt on the grass, hovering over the edges of the charts, we plotted the best course from Seattle via Victoria up to Ketchikan, and then on to Juneau: where was it best to fly over water, where to hug the shore or turn inland? The breeze caught the edges of the charts, lifting them like magic carpets or occasionally flipping them over, forcing us to grab at them to keep them from blowing into the river. From now on, I told myself, there would be other places to live, other ways of being.

In the aftermath, I would hear descriptions of myself—"unsavory," "pitiful," "foolish"—and would forget, for a moment, that people were talking about *me*. But at the time, and even afterwards, I did not care about being savory, or admirable, or savvy. I wished to be restored to myself, and to do that, if possible, by bringing someone I loved more fully into her own light. I had not been able to find a way of doing that within marriage; rather than die, I would do it outside of marriage. But once I had acknowledged this cruel survivalist streak, I left scripts behind.

In the workshop of the world, any vision of a new beginning with a new person is subject to infinite revision. Two people must find a way to mesh both lofty and mundane ways of negotiating the world—saying prayers, arguing, doing laundry—and this must happen while one or the other person is also inevitably grieving a loss, even a desired loss. The psychology of renewal is nothing like a situation comedy, and that, ironically, is its source of tragedy: many routes all lead to the same bad end. No one is clairvoyant enough to predict the route through darkness, yet almost everyone is happy to predict the end of that route—failure, overwhelming sadness, loss. This was true of most of my friends and relatives, with a few lovely exceptions. But the details of the route made it possible for me to keep on living through the loss.

What could I do, I began to ask myself, who could I be that would be better than the person I was? I sensed myself sliding, grasping for a life with this new soulmate. To her I made things "complicated," a comment I might have heard as a request to slow down, but she did not slow down, and neither did I. What followed were a series of retreats and returns, like successive tsunamis, until, waking alone in my sleeping bag in my new apartment, I began to remember what aloneness meant.

Now she and I were trying to figure out what to do, but no words came beyond the stupid platitudes I thought I would never utter. I was desperate.

"Can't we get back to the place we were before?"

"Before what?"

"Before—" I didn't know what.

"When was that, Tom?"

"You know, when we talked about Elwha and the Forest Service and places we loved most. Back then."

It was hopeless, although she had the grace to consider how a retreat might be possible. We arranged to see each other the following Sunday. Sunday morning, however, she called, sounding wiped out.

"I drank a *hell* of a lot last night," she said, "and you know why? It was you. Or us."

We talked in monosyllables of unrecognizable comfort. "Well then," I said, sitting on the floor, "maybe we should stop seeing each other."

It hung for a strange moment, like the kind of time involved in car accidents, avalanches. "I guess so," she said.

I cried when she called two days later. "I really missed talking to you," she said. "Ditto," I answered. And we talked. It was almost the way it used to be, should have been, because there was something real between us—we knew it—and we couldn't make it work. We knew that, too. Or seemed to.

We saw each other a few more times, aware each time of a toll we were taking on each other, wanting so much to be together and yet realizing a key was missing, one single channel of connection we couldn't detect among so many others coming through loud and clear. Ultimately even the words of comfort were a hurt. And yet something, still something, was there.

III

A story with no ending. Why do I think that? It's around seven o'clock now, and although the sun shows no signs of setting it hovers low enough behind the western mountains that the light here at Crow Pass becomes pale, like heather attenuated to a breeze. It is well past the bright time when the alpine meadows flood with stream violet and buttercup, oxytrope and alp lily and wallflower. The flowers now blooming carry the names of pragmatism, change, withdrawal:

fleabane, fireweed, monk's hood. Most of the landscape is given over to sturdy meadow grass and lichen. I am poor with plants, too often misidentifying them or confusing them with next-of-kin, but I would swear that I saw box saxifrage blooming at Crystal Lake on the way in. It ought to have vanished a month ago. Like a story told beyond its expected limit, the small yellow flower surprised me, as if it were living out of time.

But perhaps I was looking for omens, since what I want to do for a little while is to live out of time. That is most likely why I came here, where the weather was forecast as cloudy with a chance of heavy fog, and where I knew I was likely either to eke out a campsite between two layers of fog or lose my way in that white darkness. What I wanted was to shed my surroundings. In that brief life without context, I thought I might be able to reflect more clearly on what I had gained and lost last year, and trace the route I had instinctively taken.

I look around. It's hard not to be Biblical about a place like the Chugach mountains—they're so recent, so harsh, so sharply-etched. The mist coming up from Raven Creek creeps over the glacial silt and scree like the original mist watering the earth in Genesis, and I half-expect to see archetypal human beings, pale shades at first and then obviously substantial and wide-eyed, coming forward to greet me. But what would that make me? Something that existed before humans, before mammals? A part of the glacial moraine, the rock, the lichen? I stumble like a paleontologist onto this fantasy, instantly tracing my roots back past the Creation to an earlier time, before the God I learned in Sunday School, a time of forces and beings—the late Cretaceous period, 65 million years ago, when the Chugach terrane slammed up against north America and formed a ring of volcanoes north of here. I am among their descendents, co-existent with the mist watering the earth, but earlier, volcanic.

If I have a different origin from the one taught to me so long ago, perhaps I have a different destiny as well. What I am afraid of most is the possibility that all the volcanic upheavals of my life last year, both those that simply happened and those I set in motion, were for naught. If they were blips on the psychic register—antique neuroses claiming their due and slipping back again beneath the surface of consciousness, unexorcised—then I am relatively powerless against them, and live from day to day haunted by the possibility that their fantasies and furies drive me slowly toward destruction. But if the events of the past year are a command to pay attention to different and deeper sources, then perhaps, despite the damage I have caused, I can still learn to listen. I can listen to them, and to my farther self, and to those people who do, from time to time, come into my life to show me my failings and to show me a new way. I can live without a noose around my neck.

And this may be why I think of the story I tell myself about the woman I loved out of time as a story with no ending. No one loves out of time, and yet all true love feels as if it were. Thus all true love is a lie—but the kind of lie the poet Kenneth Fields meant when he wrote, "I have a way of telling truth with lies." There is a truth: we are transformed through love; whether we are fortunate or deeply damaged, we do not end where we begin; as someone once wrote in a moment of simple wisdom, "Love never leaves us where it found us." But the love I am remembering here is more powerful now, when time stops, because when time starts again that love seems to have no place.

The temperature has dropped perhaps twenty degrees as I've been hiking a little along the ridge, watching the mist and waiting and thinking, and although there is no sign of the night, the weather signals nightfall. I retreat to my one-person tent, a narrow shelter with a high-bowed ridge pole and a netting through which I can see the sky. Listening to the wind against the sides of the tent, I strain to hear the sounds I do not want to hear.

And then I stop. No more straining. I simply listen. I can hear the wind in the tufts of grass; I can hear the finches calling out their small finds, and if I concentrate I can hear the rush of their wings like a second wind as they fly by the tent. It strikes me suddenly that I can hear very precisely, almost as if I were the thing or the creature I am hearing. The sounds are exceptionally interesting. I hear a sparrow land on the rock just beyond my tent, hear her flutter down to the grass beside my tent, hear her test the grass for hidden food with her beak. The sound is small and clear, and different from the sound of her flying away, or the sound of the ground squirrel moving across the narrow meadow just beyond me. I am drawn outward, away from my anxieties and fears, into a world of sound and sense.

When I stop listening, I notice that the light has changed. The late evening sun is almost off the peak across from me. Rolling over to check my watch, I find that it's almost eight o'clock: I have been elsewhere, relatively speaking, for almost an hour. It seemed like a few minutes. Glancing out the door of my tent, I see the mist still concealing the valley from view. Nothing has changed, except that I have come back from the place I most wanted to be, back into the realm of ordinary thought.

"I am the bear"—I laugh at myself. What a stupid thing to think! But in that moment I willingly believed, or did more than believe—was certain, the way I might be certain about leaping safely over a three-foot crevasse or even walking down a sidewalk. And the part of me that knew this certainty could also listen for an hour to the sounds of finches and ground squirrels and the wind without getting bored or worrying about other things to do. That part of me was more connected to the world than I had ever imagined myself being.

For most of my life I believed that true journeys were spiritual and interior. They were matters of contemplation and prayer, not travel. Because I grew up learning in Christian Science that the world was spiritual, not material, the so-called material world was of no consequence to me; I sought the spirit. I sought that higher reality through prayer, through language, and through readings of events in this world that confirmed a spirit behind appearances. If anyone had asked, I would have said that the best work I could do for this world would take place in one place—a bedroom, a study, a church. I could raise up the world and heal myself of the belief of mortality without moving from one spot, if only I could learn to know God with complete devotion and humility.

Yet it was strange how much the world fascinated me. It fascinated me so much it terrified me: I was afraid of travel, almost any travel, as a child because I seemed to lose touch with my spiritual duty. The world was so big, so strange, that I began to feel myself slipping away whenever I went out in it. And this was true early on. Among my earliest memories is a short trip in a neighbor's car to the county fair, during which, when we were about halfway there, I insisted that he turn around and take me home. Though his grandkids all made fun of me, it was better than what I knew was going to happen: I was going to go out of myself, to lose control, to vomit, to pee or shit in my pants, to be hated and die of embarrassment and self-hatred.

Not much later, however, I was building scale models of space ships—the Mercury capsule, Gemini 8, and later Apollo 8—and reading up on space travel, on stars and planets, on motion. Because my religion so effectively explained the illusory nature of the world, I felt no need to study human science, and avoided it as assiduously as I could by the time I got to high school. Yet the part of me that liked to play, that imagined the adventure of motion and the secrets of sailors and rebels and buried treasure, was not assuaged by the comforts of faith. That part of me had deeper roots, and although I ignored them as long as I could, the flower they ultimately sent up was too strange and wild to be ignored. I suddenly saw what I had missed—not simply knowledge, the basic knowledge of biology and chemistry and physics, but a way of feeling at home in the world. And that was part of why, last year, I decided it would be better to die than to live in ignorance of that flower.

But I was still a person shaped by early exposure to the world as spirit, and despite my retreats and upheavals I found that I could not lay aside that vision. It remained a certainty as powerful as any I could find of my place in nature. I began to wonder, then, whether I was destined to go back, begging forgiveness from all I had offended, to those original teachings, turning my back on the world as a seduction and a cheat, writing off journeys into space or into the atom as poor imitations of God-given realities. Was that what last year had been about? I hoped not. There was always the risk that I was going to be trapped between two modes of living—one spiritual, one earthly; yet I wondered if I was somehow going to learn that the two were not, as I had been taught, mutually exclusive, but complements of the same reality. I began to see that I was going to have to undertake, not simply spiritual journeys, but physical ones: that I would have to go, and see, and be in places where by instinct I believed there might be some congruence between the inner journey and the outer one. Yet in these places, despite my instinct, I felt I could not count on a blessing. For what I had not really admitted to myself was that there were demons in my life, connected to those original religious teachings, and somehow I would have to exorcise them. What I sensed ahead was not a benign physical journey toward the spirit, but something much less abstract and much more dangerous. I did not, in all honesty, particularly want to face it.

This came to me slowly, with none of the force of a revelation, and it came to me with a sense of weariness over loss and waste, over love that I had given that had gotten lost and love given to me that I somehow could not keep. The inner and outer journeys had a romantic ring to them, but the romance rang false for me: I was on no romantic quest. The stakes were too high. I was on a quest to see if there was any reason to continue living. It was really as simple as that.

And I am here at Crow Pass because last fall, at a moment of great misery, someone came into my life who called back the childhood notions of journeying, who reminded me that the earth was not an illusion or a metaphor but a creature in its own right, containing a history of its genesis and evolution within its crust and mantle. There were more ways of thinking about the world than I had let myself imagine as an adult, and she reminded me of their reality. But it seemed that she would be neither my Virgil nor my Beatrice. To get to them, I would have to turn back into myself, and away from myself, and I would have to do this to a great extent alone.

Now, however, the easing down of night onto this volatile terrain above the mist brings an unexpected comfort, as if because I am not who I thought I was I can think my old thoughts without despair. Something moves just beyond the camp—too big for a ground squirrel, too random for a human. I think, "This is where I should stop breathing," but I don't. I sit up, listening. My head brushes the top of the tent. What should I do? Should I curl up in a ball? Play dead? Leap shouting out of the tent? Will I see the bear first, or will I simply hear the shredding of the tent as my back arcs with the agony of his claws ripping my skin? These are idle thoughts: I think how rare it is for bears to attack people without provocation, and I think beyond that of what I experienced earlier this evening, and how in a way I just don't care: if he is there, let him do what he will.

The sound fades. Perhaps it was a Dall sheep. Or perhaps it was nothing. I lie back down as old prayers come to mind—the twenty-third Psalm, a hymn I used to sing at Friends Community School in Pennsylvania, a poem by Mary Baker Eddy. I say these aloud, quietly, to the night. The more I say, the more words and music come to mind, until, in the scant darkness of midnight, I feel the tent filled with the music and language of love. And when I am lifted up among the stars, astonished at the nearness of Cassiopeia and Orion, I look back down at my dark campsite in the Chugach mountain range of Alaska and see that I have scarcely journeyed at all. Anyone can be lifted up among the stars in a dream of

Thomas Simmons

love, but what matters now, this old intuition says, is that I have left part of a world behind and have sought part of another. From now on, the real journey will not be like a dream. I fall asleep in the presence of that ursine certainty.

Coda

"From now on" is a long time to be certain of something, even with an "ursine certainty." It is early summer, 1994, almost two years after my journey through the Chugach National Forest and about a year-and-a-half after I wrote "Crow Pass, 1992." These have been eighteen months of silence—torture for a writer.

Days have passed, months: I have sat at the computer, trying to think, trying to find something to say. A few pages have come; they have all been garbage. After six months, I put the diskette and a printout of "Crow Pass, 1992" in a drawer to forget about them. Whatever hope and grief was bound up in that piece, I had to excise it from my life. I had thought I could do that by writing through, or beyond, the essay. Then I decided that that was not possible. I had to jettison the essay, to "let it go," as well-meaning people often say to the grieving.

But I couldn't jettison it, because I was not holding it; it was holding me. And I did not know why. All I knew was that my family and I had been living in Iowa for over a year, and I was beginning to feel like an automaton again, going through the motions of living and working in a surprisingly foreign place. My first two books had seemed to fall by the wayside; though they remained sources for me, they did so in difficult and complicated ways. I loved my children; and, along with my wife, I found an ironic strength in our proximity to divorce. But otherwise it was difficult for me to point to anything that felt like a locus of power or health. I began to have nightmares of repeating my fate at MIT—and worse, of repeating it because I had not learned something I thought I had learned from that fateful autumn of 1991, when in an act of desperation I tried to define more clearly for myself who I was. Had I been in full retreat from myself since then, because what had happened then was simply too painful to bear? Would that be the pattern—desperate measures, full retreats?

Thinking like this is a way of closing even the smallest windows on one's own hope. I began to wake up once again in the middle of the night, dreading the arrival of the day. In a milder act of desperation, parallel to the fall of 1991 but quite distant from it, I dug through my files around Christmas 1993 to find the Crow Pass essay. And then I began to read.

For weeks that essay was all I read outside of the books and student essays I'd assigned for my classes. I'd carry pages of the essay around with me, pondering them, even laughing at them. I filled the margins with comments to myself. At one point, re-reading my thumbnail description of loss near the beginning of the essay, I stopped at the line "I had lost someone else very precious to me, someone I imagined to be intimately in my future"; it was a line that had left me feeling physically cold every time I read it. But to imagine a self connected to my future, I now wrote to myself, I had to have had some sense of a "me" at the time I wrote the essay; who was that? Obviously I did not know the answer—either in my own life or in the essay. But did that mean that our selves were always unknown? Was there any such thing as a "self"? I understood at least that I had to speak to myself in a language that made sense to me, and the world "self" made a certain kind of sense. There might be many versions of this self, but they constituted or ought to constitute a discrete identity, something I could point to as a way of separating me from other people and from former versions of me that I no longer found supportable. At least that was my intuition about this language.

The questions mounted: "Who are you," I asked myself in the essay, "and what do you love?" It was impossible, I wrote to myself in the margins, to answer the first question except by answering the second. But what did I love? I loved conflicting things: I loved two people who spoke to very different sides of my life; I loved different parts of the world, different places where I imagined myself to be fully rooted; I loved differing ideas of faith; I even loved differing ideas about love, what love was or could be. At one point I leaned back in my chair, the essay in hand, and I simply allowed myself to feel a deepening burden of hopelessness. Who could love me, or even trust me, knowing how torn I was as a human being? Who could risk being with me, knowing that I was as devoted to physical wilderness as I was to transcendent spirituality, as I was to my children, as I was even—in a strange, unlikely way—to marriage? I was a disaster as a human being.

But having said this, I began to recover something from "Crow Pass," something about learning to live through the disastrousness of one's own humanity by looking for points of contact between the animal or natural world and the world of spirit. Perhaps that contact was a vain assumption, but it was *my* assumption—the only one I had found comforting on those four days of intense writing in late December 1992, with Lesley and the kids off to visit friends in St. Louis and me sitting at the kitchen table, computer keyboard beneath my fingers, photographs of the Crow Pass trail scattered around me, along with various books and topographical maps. It was true: I no longer wanted to be human, if being human meant what I had been for 36 years. Being human was too horrible, too full of pain received and unintentional pain inflicted, too rooted in suffering, too full of impenetrable mystery. But what if, implicit in the human experience, was the possibility of moving beyond that kind of humanity?

Humans were not simply creatures of powerful imaginations, but of yearnings that could translate into reality: that, at least, was a message I had absorbed from my strange upbringing, and it came through now as a message of health. Christian Scientists were not the only religious people to believe that they could heal through their faith—or could radically transform their sense of the reality of the world. Early Hasidic Jews—of whom, as A.N. Wilson writes, Jesus was probably one—practiced charismatic healing; the Navajo had spiritual seers or singers whose many "ways" still lead to healings of many kinds of trauma; even fundamentalist Protestants, with whom I imagine myself having virtually nothing in common, have reimagined themselves through acts of faith so powerful that they can, for example (as in a film sequence almost too carefully documented by the *60 Minutes* investigative team) drink apparently lethal poison without harm to themselves. It wasn't so much physical healing I sought, however, but a new identity—or rather, an identity that could accommodate the intensity of my time at Crow Pass without feeling obliged to retreat.

I have not been back to Alaska since August of 1992. Whenever I have planned a trip there, its associations have proved explosive, as if whoever I was trying to be was not yet coherent enough to make use of a return. And the time away has grown increasingly complicated. Recently I have awakened several times in the middle of the night with deep pains in my stomach, after having dreams in which I am diagnosed with stomach cancer. As I lie in bed, sweating, trying not to wake my wife, who lies in a peaceful sleep beside me, I work my way back into the dream and realize how much the dream was associated with passionlessness: how I wept in one dream because I had lost all passion for living; how I raged in another, and moved far away to a place where I was alone and could await the arrival of one who knew the other side of my life, and could heal me from that side. These were desperate dreams, and I have no antidote for them: no antidote but writing, and a return to Crow Pass—certainly in words, and perhaps, in the end, in body as well.

The undercurrent of all my dreams is the mortal danger of living a lie. But what constitutes that lie—and what is the countervailing truth? Who are you, and what do you love? If those questions still prove in some ways too frightening, it is also clearly important to track their corollaries: what do you hate? What repulses you or makes you despair? For in both these questions there is passion, and passion is the "ursine certainty" I spoke of so long ago—not a wild passion, necessarily bent on destruction, but a fierce confidence in the rightness of living, a confidence so powerful that it may finally surpass language or the meditation that precedes it. Animal consciousness and spiritual consciousness conjoin in this confidence, I think, although I am only guessing with the kind of instinctual hope that makes me glad I am still an animal. I will go back among the animals, I tell myself; but to reach them I must go back through the human animals, whom I know least well of all.

Thomas Simmons

The Garden

On my mother's wall is a saying from Isaac Bashevis Singer's *Zlateh the Goat and Other Stories*. "In stories time does not vanish," it says. "Neither do men and animals. For the writer and his readers all creatures go on living forever. What happened long ago is still present.

"It is in this spirit that I wrote these tales. In real life many of the people that I describe no longer exist, but to me they remain alive and I hope they will amuse the reader with their wisdom, their strange beliefs, and sometimes with their foolishness."

Above the saying is Maurice Sendak's etching of Zlateh and Aaron, the boy who discovered that he and the goat could save each other's lives. The story goes like this. Aaron's father Reuven, the town furrier, orders Aaron to sell Zlateh to the butcher so that the family will have food to eat and presents for the children during Hanukkah. But a mighty blizzard descends as Aaron and Zlateh walk to the butcher's, and they very nearly lose their lives. At the last possible moment, Aaron finds a haystack in which they can take refuge. Zlateh eats the hay and keeps Aaron alive with her milk until the storm passes. In the end, the grieving family is so overjoyed to find Aaron alive that they lose all thought of slaughtering Zlateh, and the natural grace of the world descends upon them so that they lack for nothing during Hanukkah.

To me, who grew up believing in the healing power of religious faith, this is a story of healing. But it is also, first, a *story* –with characters who existed in a book, on my mother's wall, and finally in my world—and, I suspect, in hers. The saying and Sendak etching are as original as they can be, which is to say that the etching is a print from Sendak's original plate, and the quotation from Singer is handset in a typeface I should know but don't, though it may be Caslon or Cheltenham Old Style. This is one of my mother's most prized possessions, not only because it is both beautiful and valuable but because it was given to her by an artist and teacher she understood to be great—a man named Tom Bostelle. I was a young child on the day he brought it to her, but I remember witnessing the exchange at the back door of our Pennsylvania house—the etching for a glass of lemonade and a few words of conversation.

When we moved to California in 1969, my mother hung this framed etching on the kitchen wall above her small desk across from the cabinet where we kept cereal and baking pans. The space she considered hers in this house was about thirty square feet—that is, about five feet by six feet—but it was a kind of magic circle, with Singer and Sendak and, by implication, Bostelle in the center. We knew that she would write in her voluminous diaries here, once the family had left the house early in the morning, and she would have this space to herself until we returned from school or work.

The Sendak etching hangs on a very pale blue wallpaper with blue and red and yellow flowers intertwining wherever they are not interrupted by cabinets and appliances. My mother chose this wallpaper because it made the kitchen an extension of the only part of the house beyond the kitchen that really mattered, which was the garden. Arriving somewhat by accident in a part of the world we knew nothing about, we quickly discovered that houses could, in California, be mere extensions of gardens. Half of the back wall of our house was plate glass, and it opened out onto a rose garden and a small grove of three cherry trees and one plum tree and one pear tree and one loquat tree, along with a young Monterey pine and several eucalyptus trees, as foreign to us as Australia, and a series of small paths defined with cedar borders and tanbark, which snaked among these trees and among other plants, the beautiful, poisonous oleander and the daphne and the ivy, and many others the names of which I did not know and would never know. In moving to California we had moved to a private garden, and when we went indoors it was only to sleep or to change our clothes or, sometimes, to eat.

I spend, and have spent, much time in this garden. Although the tanbark trails cannot be more than a hundred yards long altogether, I walk among them for an hour at a time, observing the shifting patterns of light on leaf and vine, checking the progress of these most delicious plums, noticing that I too change as I move though this lush plateau—becoming more subversive and piratical as I move into the thick growth of manzanita and other native foliage, becoming more quiet and Edenic as I move out into the open, onto the tiny meadow between the cherry trees. Everywhere here is abundance, but also strange varieties of light and color and shade, as sensual to me as the skin of a plum or the meat of a pear or a loquat, but more transient, more malleable, more like a story. There are many kinds of light here, and there are many of me, and all of us spend much time watching the light change us. We make up many stories here.

I was only a moderate reader as a child, and what I read divided largely into four categories: *Archie* and *Sad Sack* comics; *The Hardy Boys*; Stephen W. Meader adventures stories (because he was a resident of the New Jersey town in which I'd spent some summers); and the encyclopedia. I read most of these before our move to California, and while I read much more in high school, I read erratically (the works of Henry James one summer, for example, while sitting on an inflatable yellow raft in the middle of a swimming pool) and I read outdoors. Indoors, at night and in the winter, I preferred to do what I had always done in Pennsylvania, which was to watch TV. Like many kids I watched as much *Star Trek* as I could. My favorite device was the transporter: it always fascinated me to see the shimmering light preceding the arrival of a body. And every now and

Thomas Simmons

then, the body did not arrive, and that particular *Star Trek* episode would be made complete by the destruction of one of its parts, its creatures.

This story is complete in the same way. For the Los Altos wall, which no longer exists, on which my mother, long dead, hung an etching which has since been lost—all of this now begins to shimmer, and the effect is not the mere self-consciousness of writing, of wanting to draw a brief essay to a close (in order to say, if nothing else, "I am a writer"), but an anxiety about what it means for so much to exist without space or time, transported into the inner molecular space of memory—one memory. Is there a collective and personal unconsious, the Tantric "indestructible drop," where nothing dies? My old friend and antagonist Robert Pinsky once wrote a poem about this, called "The Garden."

> Far back, in the most remote times with their fresh colors,
> Already and without knowing it I must have begun to bring
> Everyone into the shadowy garden—half-overgrown,
>
> A kind of lush, institutional grounds—
> Singly or in groups, into that green recess. Everything
> Is muffled there; they walk over a rich mulch
>
> Where I have conducted them together into summer shade
> And go on bringing them, all arriving with no more commotion
> Than the intermittent rustling of birds in the dense leaves,
>
> Or birds' notes in chains or knots that embroider
> The sleek sounds of water bulging over the dam's brim:
> Midafternoon voices of chickadee, kingbird, catbird;
>
> And the falls, hung in a cool, thick nearly motionless sheet
> From the little green pond to shatter perpetually in mist
> Over the streambed. And like statuary of dark metal
>
> Or pale stone around the pond, the living and the dead,
> Young and old, gather where they are brought: some nameless;
> Some victims and some brazen conquerors; the shamed and the haunters;
>
> The harrowed; the cherished; the banished—or mere background figures,
> Old men from a bench, girl with glasses from school—all brought beyond
> Even memory's noises and rages, here in the quiet garden.

In this poem it is the poet who, "without knowing it," arranges for the arrival of all those who have peopled his world, the loved and the shamed and those who haunt them—but he takes them somewhere that cannot exist in the world, as a way of showing how consciousness, which is the locus of the world in memory, might transcend itself.

It's strange freight, consciousness: we know its strangeness; many of us would rather be something other than conscious, although it's an unwritten rule of the species that we don't say this to each other unless we're crazy or clinically depressed. Those of us who tell stories may do so in part because it allows us to be someone else or even, if we are very good at it, to be selves whose closest relations are not other humans but rather other creatures, or plants, or stones (I once had a very gifted student who explained in an essay that, during her childhood, her closest confidante had been a small, salmon-colored boulder named Hildegard, hidden in a field of corn). Stepping into the shimmering light, knowing we may never return, we see—what?—a garden? Perhaps not; perhaps something darker. But Eden was a garden; and the wall of my mother's house, with its quilted flowers, was a garden; and Zlateh the goat came to live in that garden; and I assume now that such a garden is still possible, and that at some time in my life when truly nothing happens, which may or may not be when I am dead, I will walk back into that garden and see what it is that Singer now knows, what Tom Bostelle was trying to tell my mother, what my mother was trying to tell me, what I cannot tell you.

Thomas Simmons

Shotgun

I wake in the morning and look out the window. My wife wakes up. My son is already awake upstairs, watching cartoons on the TV; my daughter is still sleeping. From the window I can see workmen arriving at the new apartment complex across the street. They will soon be busy wrapping the outside of the building in a kind of impermeable plastic sheathing, applying vinyl siding, putting up drywall inside, painting, putting up cabinets. Gathering my clothes, I get dressed, then climb the stairs to the main floor of our small house, where I fix breakfast for my son; my wife goes in to wake our daughter.

This is the beginning of our day, of our many days, many of them virtually identical in appearance, and not significantly different from the days of our neighbors. If there is such a thing as a neighborhood rhythm, we are part of it. And although this is new neighborhood, a vinyl haven (as I say jokingly to my sister in Maine), designed for people with rocky pasts to gain a toehold in the real estate market, it is already *real:* it rises indisputably from the surface of the greened earth, infused with decorative shrubs and marigolds and gardens, with Hyundais and Kawasakis and Bayliners and Duplos. It is solid and substantial.

Almost every morning, however, it strikes me as peculiar how much this neighborhood and its rhythms, and those of the workmen across the street, and the neighbors on the other side of them, and the more prosperous people with somewhat different rhythms across the big highway in the town, and those even more prosperous people on the other side of town—how all of this depends not on things or even, strictly speaking, on people, but on our shared consciousness of the basic fables: fables of struggle, labor, stability, satisfaction, pleasure. What if we begin to think, however, that struggle, labor, stability, satisfaction, and pleasure are not givens? What if we begin to suspect that—unlike housewrap—these categories are not impervious to mildew or rot or parasites, but might actually be tilted, tipped over, dropped, transformed through great discipline or great trauma, or even abandoned? What happens when we begin to think of consciousness itself as something fragile?

These past few mornings I have awakened thinking of two sentences from James Galvin's *The Meadow*. He is writing about the brothers and sister of Lyle, one of the central characters in the book. One brother, an Army pilot, is killed in World War II; another brother, who takes up cropdusting, dies by snagging his plane "on a powerline in Texas before he'd been at it a year." Two tragedies in a short span of time. And then a third: "Then Clara started automatic writing and pretty soon she was hearing voices. The voices told her to take Lyle's rifle and put it in her mouth."

I have never heard voices, although I have sometimes referred to "voices" in my writing as a way of describing strong insights, which I take to be instinctive and true, directing me toward something I need. But these are not, apparently, the kind of voices Clara heard. And yet I can well imagine the impossibility of ridding one's mind of them, once they arrive. To have one's mind divided against itself—how do you take sides? How do you stand up to whatever part of it seems (to another part) outrageous, and say, "I am not you—I cannot be you—I cast you out?" Isn't that what Clara did, in fact—only she wound up on what we'd call the wrong side?

Taking "sides," trusting one "part" against another "part"—even the language breaks down here. For this is not simply a hemispheric discussion, not a matter of left brain and right brain duking it out for the trophy of sanity. It is, of course, something much subtler, perhaps synaptic, perhaps induced—as it apparently was, in "part," for Clara, and as it was for me as well—by long, difficult circumstances with a few extremities thrown in.

One of the consequences, for me, of growing up in a religion that emphasized the spiritual perfection of the universe was that I could not trust my own perceptions or insights. "Everything real is eternal," Mary Baker Eddy said, and I was to seek out the real because it was eternal. As a spiritual idea, I was already at home in the eternal universe of the spirit. But who was this "I"? It appeared to be a mortal body, with a mortal brain, and taste, touch, smell, sight, and sound. Yet I learned in Sunday School that all of these were lies, falsifications of my true identity. Still: to get through a day I had to trust the lies. I had to trust them without thinking about them, even as I told myself that my true self lived in a higher reality. But what happened when I did think about them? What was the nature of the alternative unreality which they were giving me?

I began asking these questions, not out of intellectual curiosity, but out of a profound sense that something had been wrong in my life from the earliest years of memory. One day when I was seven years old, for example, I cried hysterically from about noon until bedtime (what must my mother and father have thought?) because I'd learned that I needed glasses, and glasses to me were an outward confirmation—evidence *to the world*—that I was not perfect and spiritual, but imperfect and mortal. People would be able to see that I could not see; they could see that I had failed as a spiritual idea. And yet, when I finally got these heavy, ugly, black-framed glasses with glass lenses that would break with only a little coaxing, I saw things I had never seen before: the stars; cracks in the ceiling in my school classroom; my dog running toward me from across the yard; a lone swimmer in the ocean. If I had failed as a spiritual idea, why was I being rewarded for this failure by seeing? How could it be that my punishment was to be rewarded? Did that mean that I had fully succumbed to the lie of the mortal world? Was I being drawn away from the spirit, despite the best efforts of my parents and their Christian Science practitioner? If so, what had I done wrong? What had I done, in my seven years, to make God reject me?

The mindset here, which I would say is endemic to any religion which absolutely rejects the nature of the world into which we are born, is a mindset ripe for serious mental illness—for depression or, indeed, schizophrenia. And it may be that I have been depressed for many years. But more frightening than this was a time, now nearly fifteen years ago, when I began to believe that things had happened which had not happened, and that I had done things I had not done. This, I now suspect (for it has been beyond the ability of any therapist I have seen to make this clear to me), was in a strange way an impulse toward health on the part of my psyche. Wanting to be whole, to live in a coherent universe, my psyche punished me by making me believe I had sinned against the spirit in specific ways. Though I had no recollection of it, I had, I believed, had sex with various women (I know; how quaint this sounds now! But I had an upbringing 100 years older than the generation in which I actually lived); I had, I believed, even murdered people without remembering it.

That first fear, of sexual license, held great sway for me, for sexuality was an ultimate *non sequitur*, the equivalent for twenty-year-old of the seven-year-old's glasses. Through my experience of generous and loving sexuality, I saw that the mortal world could be very beautiful. And this was an "error," an acceptance of the unreal as real; therefore I had to be punished for it. Since an attraction to the unreal meant that I had abandoned the real—including real cause and effect—I condemned myself to a totally amoral universe, in which I could not really predict or know what I did, and in which I might well be a murderer simply because that was the kind of world in which I'd chosen to live.

It is horrible to read back over this sickness, to know how many years it was brewing in my mind as I attended Sunday School and memorized the books of the Bible and studied Mary Baker Eddy's *Science and Health with Key to the Scriptures*. When this sickness emerged, it came like a devil, and there were whole days—whole days—when I wanted to rip my mind out of my skull to get these thoughts to stop. Nevertheless, some part or dimension of my mind resisted this, and recognized my religiously-induced obsessions as an overlay, a growth like an unresolved grief, and knew that the overlay was false. It *was* possible to live with beauty and compassion and gracefulness and joy in this world, I heard myself say; God will not punish you for believing this. But this answer was too simple, and on days when the dark version was strong I could almost feel the two sides battling in my mind, until I was exhausted from the fight and could not walk or eat or even get out of bed.

But I survived. And I survived with a sense of consciousness as a darkness, an outgrowth of the crust and mantle of the earth, right at first because it is what it is, instinctive and true, but then, almost imperceptibly and routinely, damaged by contact with higher "realities"—with rituals, with community, with money, with school, with work, with religion. Of course, this contact is unavoidable, and it is the embodiment of bleakness (or radical romanticism) to suggest that all of our human intercourse destroys the powerful source from which we emanate. But I don't mean that, exactly. I was fortunate to keep believing, even in my darkest times, that the source to which I was linked even before birth, even before conception, was there and real, that it was of this earth, and that the whole essence of its being was to direct, to guide, to illuminate with darkness. I was its creature, not anyone else's; and as lonely and as isolated and tormented as I might be, that truth would never change. It was something for me to hang onto (and may explain, in passing, my intermittently passionate interest in paleontology and geology).

I have only once seen a suicide by gunshot. This was in the summer of 1971, when I was 15 and worked at Cox Cameras in Mountain View, California. At the time, the Mountain View police department did some of its photo finishing with us, and we were supposed to check through each roll to make sure the negatives had been developed correctly and the quality of the prints was acceptable. Most of these were photographs of routine police work—minor to moderate auto accidents, broken windows or door locks, or other evidence of burglary. One day, however, my colleague Pauline motioned me over to the side counter. She was an interesting character, having had a rough childhood and having made her way through the world largely on her own cunning; she loved parties and violence. "Wanna see something really gross?" she asked. Before I could answer, she handed me a stack of black-and-white pictures. It took me a second to figure out the top one. I saw first a room with walls, and feet connected to legs connected to a torso, and a shotgun between the legs, and arms at the side of the torso—but the head: there was a kind of distorted chin, and then nothing, or rather a kind of wide, not-quite-shapeless mush, and the wall behind this object looked like magazine illustrations I had seen of the first three minutes of the universe, in which an explosive cloud of gas had scattered debris outward with fundamental force. Then I realized what I was seeing.

"Blew his head off," Pauline said. I hadn't realized she was looking over my shoulder. "You ever seen anything like that?"

I hadn't. Mechanically, I looked through the stack: picture after picture, from the front, from the side, from above—a particularly gruesome angle, particularly humiliating—and all this black-and-white blood and brains decorating an otherwise-undecorated apartment wall in Mountain View. I wondered what this man had done, what he had been, who had loved him, who had hated him, what women or men had called him a fucking asshole and how many of them had done that, how many jobs he had lost, how much his father or his mother's boyfriends had beaten him, whether he had a father, whether his mother had cried herself to sleep in the room next to him or in the same room...unsubstantiated questions with no answers, and all this wondering in a few seconds' time. Until that moment I didn't really understand what it meant to commit suicide. The pictures of that man, with his brains shot out of his open head like worms and interstellar cranial matter spattered all over the wall, have never lost their power. It is now 1994, and I remember those photographs as if I still held them in my dampening hand.

For whatever reason, I have so far never been much attracted by suicide. Still, I understand the combat between those little-understood "parts" of the mind, and I sense the power of directives for that man, and for Clara, who could hear no other way out. The intuitive voice of the earth, which I claim for myself, is not the voice that everyone claims; it may be, in fact, that we acquire health only as we identify our central source and inspiration as fundamentally private, impervious to the damage we live through unknowingly for years in the earliest part of our lives. If that is true, I cannot speculate on the deepest privacies of the man's suicide, or of Clara's, and I cannot know if they ever had countervailing forces that finally became too dim, too inaudible, and faded the way Devonian coral or trilobites fade under the constant footsteps of human tourists. To the extent that we are all exhibitions in the tours of other human beings, we run an enormous risk of losing our origins. Who knows if, for suicides, the voices telling them to leave are not, at some level over which we despair, voices of health, insisting on an end to this life when the primary umbilical cord—the one that exists before birth, before conception, though it is nevertheless creaturely—is somehow severed?

Yet I continue to awaken each morning, in this vinyl haven, listening to my son watching cartoons upstairs, the very cartoons I watched on TV when I was his age, listening to my wife and daughter and the workmen across the street and the cars leaving their garages for commuting, for work; and I think, now, of Clara, the voices in her head and the gun in her mouth, and I think of the dead man I saw when I was 15, and I look back now, past my corrupting religion to the incorruptible earth and the God of the rocks, because I know that my own source, too, grows more faint as I grow older, and because, though I may end up blind, I try still to refuse deafness as I try still to refuse death by my own hand.

Backbone

What brings us here? I begin to understand what it means to be an eccentric, and yet an eccentric is usually someone whose eccentricity merely magnifies "ordinary" people's deepest frustrations or hopes...

For example: my family and I are at Backbone State Park, the first state park in Iowa, founded in 1919. We're about 10 miles north of Manchester, which is about 45 miles west of Dubuque, which you can find on a map if you look. It's the second time we've camped together at an official campground, and the first time in Iowa. There are 128 campsites, and on this Saturday evening in early June, virtually every site is taken. Backbone is primarily a tent campground, which I take to be a good sign on philosophical principles—few RV behemoths with air conditioning, full bathrooms, and color TV (although my son Nathaniel, as it turns out, is coveting one very comfortable-looking RV near us), but rather a bunch of tents whose owners must want to be closer to the ground, to the sound of acorns falling in the evening air, to the feel of the warm, humid air through the netting.

Still, there are contradictions: our two tents stand out because they are backpacking tents, low and light and portable, designed for trips into the Olympic peninsula or the North Cascades or Chugach National Forest. Virtually everyone else's tent is what we've come to learn is a classic midwestern campground tent: 64 to 120 feet square, a good six feet tall, with external metal supports. They're tents you can walk around in, eat in, even watch TV in (the people across from us have brought a battery-powered TV for their tent—so much for my prejudice about RV's). Another contradiction: we're here, I take it, to be out in nature, but I begin to realize that people here are quite close together, and from what I can tell they seem to like it that way. As I walk from campsite to campsite, eyeing everyone's various set-ups, I see that many of these people have rooted themselves in what is effectively a weekend tent city. They have one or more tents: sometimes a tent for sleeping in, complete with folding cots and folding chairs and a Coleman lantern, and a tent for cooking and eating in, which is not so much a tent as four walls of netting with a nylon roof, enclosing a full-size fold-up metal picnic table (usually with a blue-and-white checkered table cloth), more folding chairs, and a large hamper full of plates and utensils; big fires in the metal-lined fire pits, although it's still 80 degrees at 5 o'clock and the air is filling with a heavy haze; hammocks strung from trees; clotheslines; chaises longues; and various athletic equipment.

Standing at the edge of the campground, with a narrow strip of forest to my left and the park lake, invisible but present, just beyond that, I wonder what's natural here. Of course the answer is "humans": the humans are the nature, vast beneath the cottonwood trees tall enough to be almost unnoticeable. I notice that virtually no one looks up, even when a sunset of enormous power blazes through the western edge of the trees and foliage, as bright as the lights of the alien ship in *E. T.*.

And I'm confused, I admit, about what I feel. My wife and children are having a good time, I think. I have already taken them to the lake, where Georgia and Lesley splashed in the wading area while I took Nathaniel out on a rented paddle boat. Now, after several trips back and forth to the bathroom (complete with showers), they clearly like watching everyone else here—watching their games, their fires, their lives. Camping here is a spectator sport, but what I usually call "nature" is not the spectacle. The people, including my family, come here to run around, to make noise, to set up shop, to hang out, to be somewhere other than home, to rough it without any real loss of possessions, to watch each other. They're having fun.

Why, then, as darkness begins to fall, do I feel increasingly like a curmudgeon? With Lesley and Georgia already asleep in one tent, and Nathaniel asleep next to me in my tent, I lie awake and listen. In fact, I lie awake because I cannot possibly sleep. The noise here is, to me, overwhelming, and it is psychic as well as audible noise, and it is sad. Almost everyone is drinking. The two families next to me are going over the same family stories, kidding about how little beer will be in the case the next morning. As time goes on their judgments settle into monosyllables, single sentences: "I know she's that way. I just know it." "He won't change." They evince a strained, hopeless certainty in what they say, and I hear a bitterness I have not heard in them before. Behind me, a man and his friends (ironically, he happens to be a colleague of Lesley's, although he seems embarrassed to find us in the same park with him—what are, after all, the odds of that?—and politely avoids us) slip into a tense, endless laughter—always the same in cadence and volume: "HA-ha-ha, HA-HA-ha-ha-ha." Over and over, between inaudible words, this thin, machine-gun-like laughter blankets the park. Some time after midnight, a truck pulls up next to their camp; a park ranger steps out to have a few words with them; but they continue anyway, as before, until a little after 3 A.M.

Smoke from 75 or 80 fires hangs in the humid air, making it slightly hard to breathe. The man across the narrow camp road from me may have a mild cold or allergies: he coughs every 30 seconds or so, a cough as consistent as the laughter from the other campers—"aHUUGH aHUUGH (one-second pause), aHUUGH aHUUUGH aHUUGH." He does this from about 8 o'clock until around 4 in the morning, when I finally fall into a fitful sleep. When I awaken at 7, he is still coughing exactly the same way; I assume he did it all night. He and his wife have an infant with them, a fussy infant who cannot sleep: her wailing is incessant, the cry of a tiny, fevered animal. And then, up the hill slightly, one campsite over, the man and the woman who should not be together, but still are, and who have had too much beer, begin their slow, three-hour verbal assault on one another.

Their tone is so worn down, so faint, that at first I think they are just talking—the kind of talking the old man and woman do in Elizabeth Bishop's poem "The Moose," a kind of comfortable taking-stock. But no. His voice rises. "I'm gonna," he says. "I'm gonna." "No you ain't," she says. "Don't you touch me." I try to think what to do if this turns into a rape or a violent fight. But she holds her own, in an odd way; he backs off. There are whispered silences, then tired half-explosions: "You never ast me," she says. "You never ast me a fuckin' question." "Fuck if I don't," he says. "No, fuck you," she says, "You fuckin' don't." The talk ranges beyond sex to jobs, to the future, to the two of them. "You din't hear a fuckin' word I said," she says. "I'm gonna sleep in the truck." "No you ain't," he says. "Don't you get outta this tent." "Fuck you, I'm leavin'." "Don't you fuckin' leave." And on and on, not with any particular passion, but more like a play that has run so long that the principal players have no more enthusiasm to show, though they long ago learned their lines by heart.

The background for this, although it is not by any means background, is a child with night terrors across the campground, whose eerie shrieks sound of some deeply imagined torture, of legs broken slowly or repeatedly or of arms or torsos burned with cigarettes, or of worse things which may or may not have happened. The shrieking does not stop.

In the thickening air, in the palpable weariness that has nothing to do with physical exertion, in the sadness and futility, I feel the human weight come down hard on me. I have no safety in this tent, with my dear son sleeping next to me, and with my small gathering of equipment whose associations are all of solitude and adventure—backpacking in Alaska, in the Pacific northwest, in California. I, too, am implicated here, part of this human gathering which on this night *is* nature. This implication brings me suddenly back to the work of Joseph de Maistre, an 18th-century French reactionary philosopher, born in 1753 in Chambery, and thus fated to witness the French Revolution as a seasoned adult.

De Maistre comes to mind not simply because, in this tent-city from which I cannot escape until morning (because my family is happily sleeping, and I will not disturb them with a sudden departure—is that my weakness?), I seek refuge in intellect; I could seek refuge in far more comforting domains (by playing through my mind, for example, Ernest Bloch's "Sacred Service" or Joni Mitchell's "Blue"). But I suspect de Maistre comes to mind because, by rights, he and I ought to have nothing in common. He was an arch-royalist and a Catholic, a staunch defender of the monarchy; he had a visceral and intellectual horror of republicanism (or what we, eliding the difference, tend to call "democracy"); he had no use for Rousseauian romanticism (or for romanticism of any kind); he thought natural science was a sham, a linguistic construct rather than, strictly speaking, a method. I am more a fan of romanticism than I commonly admit, and despite doubts of various kinds I still trust scientific empiricism, though I do not necessarily "believe" in it. And when anti-authoritarian brains got handed out, I must have received a double share. What fascinates me about de Maistre, however, is his unequivocal acuteness of perception. It is death and destruction, not love, that characterizes human life, he writes. "[Man] kills to obtain food and he kills to clothe himself," de Maistre writes; "he kills to adorn himself; he kills in order to attack and he kills to defend himself; he kills to instruct himself and he kills to amuse himself; he kills to kill." Humankind, for de Maistre, has divine origins, but it is empirically evil and incredibly destructive. Unless it subjects itself to absolute authority, it stands no chance of governing itself, for its passions and irrationality will inevitably lead it into the most extended and degrading forms of misery.

What he saw and heard forms a backdrop for what I am hearing now: the strange and virtually inexplicable cries of human beings who left their homes to leave their ordinary lives, and yet, by virtue of gathering together in one small place, have intensified their ordinariness, their anxiety, their misery, even as they make it clear through their possessions that this kind of excursion is a commonplace source of hope for them, worth the expenditure of considerable sums of money. The nature, or what I call nature, that is all around them has no healing power; they are who they are here, only more so. And their fires are the fires that such an artist as Francis Ford Coppola might have created, to announce the gateway from this world to a world whose Dantean aspects are too near for comfort.

I can do nothing about this. I cannot sleep; and when I attempt to pray for the people around me, insisting on the presence of a divine comfort even here, my prayers collapse on the daggers of "fuck you!" or the wailings from far corners or the smell of smoke, and I grow angry, until even de Maistre is not enough and I find myself thinking of Jonah, who having prayed to God and having been released from the belly of the great fish, grew angry at God for saving the city of Ninevah. "Therefore now, O Lord," Jonah cries out in a fury when God shows mercy to Ninevah, "take, I beseech thee, my life from me; for it is better for me to die than to live."

Jonah goes out to the edge of the city to sit; "And the Lord God prepared a gourd [tree], and made it to come up over Jonah, that it might be a shadow over his head." Jonah is grateful for the shade; but the next day, God destroys the gourd, and Jonah is sad. But God says: "Thou has had pity on the gourd, for the which thou hast not labored, neither madest it grow; which came up in a night, and perished in a night: And should I not spare Ninevah, that great city, wherein are more than sixscore thousand persons that cannot discern between their right hand and their left hand; and also much cattle?"

In the morning, when Nathaniel and I awaken, we are greeted with a fine dusting of ash on our tent and, when we climb out of the tent, on our bodies.

Most of our neighbors are burning their trash, since the park prohibits the dumping of "private garbage" in the dumpsters near the front of the campground. Many of the fires around the camp are blazing, far higher and brighter than they were in the night, and their residue floats over all of us like the fine debris of fallen bodies. The air here is cluttered with ash. The man across from us is coughing harder. I think, then, of the irrationality of forgiveness, which Jonah so clearly felt: for who would want to forgive creatures so wounding and so wounded, so careless for themselves and for others, so casually destructive? God demonstrates that Jonah is capable of compassion—despite his relative powerlessness—by revealing to him his sorrow over the loss of a work of "nature," a tree. But Jonah's sorrow has little to do with human compassion. One might read it as a selfish sorrow—Jonah has lost the shade that shields him from the desert sun—or as a sorrow for a work of nature, beautiful in its *separateness* from humanity. Still, God observes that, whatever form Jonah's sorrow takes, God's is greater; the suffering will continue, the cries and terrors and wantonness of the people of Ninevah will continue, until some at least turn to a voice that is always there, and hear in it the presence of grace.

But what can that grace be, I ask myself, in this ashen place? My neighbors are busy with their morning breakfasts, or packing up their camps, or re-arranging them for another day's stay. They have the intractable busyness of people for whom the night was just another ordinary night in a string of ordinary nights. And I know what I want to think: I want to be ashamed of my own judgment. Who am I to pray for these people or for me, or to think of us as needing forgiveness? If they ease the strain of their lives through sleepless laughter and verbal assaults and tears, what is that to me? They are awake now, functional, no longer laughing oddly or fighting or crying; was their night away from home not, then, a good thing? God pursued Jonah, and Jonah was first afraid, then hard-hearted. God wished him to overcome both, though as it turned out the hard-heartedness was harder to cure than the fear.

It is the dawn of another day, when the smoke rises higher than the trees and diffuses the sun. A cinder gets in my eye, forcing me to blink with pain, and when I look down I see a little piece of plasticized or waxed cardboard, from a TV dinner or butter box. Yellow and red and white and singed, it will lie on the ground until the wind blows it into the woods or the lake. I remember then that Jonah was not simply hard-hearted but revolted, full of rage at Ninevah, and it was the rage that frightened God. But no God descends here to guide me, as far as I can tell, and my own anger remains whole and volatile. I can think of nothing else to do, and so I rush my family through breakfast, break camp, and drive away.

Thomas Simmons

Love

[According to Paul, Jesus] exemplified and set forth a principle of the universe: that is, that in defiance of all the cruelty of men and the indifference of nature, the principle of life itself was love.

—*A. N. Wilson,* Jesus: A Life

Although I am not by nature a birdwatcher, I have recently taken to watching the birds that come to the feeder on our upstairs porch. Because the feeder has only been in place for about three months, I see mostly the ubiquitous and adventurous species. Finches come most often; the ugly, irridescent blackbirds; then the beautiful cardinals, both male and female, and every now and then a red-winged blackbird, sportier than the raciest sports car. It is the finches I watch most often, however, and not because they are the most plentiful.

Finches interest me because the amount of seed they waste—speaking in human terms—is extraordinary, especially in comparison to their body size. Where cardinals or blackbirds will gently flick away a few seeds at the top of the feeder, almost as a polite gesture, to get to the seed below, the finches blow seeds out of the feeder as if with a machine gun. The seed goes everywhere! Flinging their beaks left and right with the energy of aerobics instructors, they pepper the porch with their leavings, so that the wooden deck looks a little like an enormous seed-covered suet stick or one of those frightening treats you see on the back of Rice Krispies cereal boxes. Finches can waste a pound to two pounds of seed a day; we buy a 25-pound bag every 10 to 14 days, knowing a good half of it will wind up on the porch or the ground below.

Although it's my money the finches consume with their seed antics, and given my temperament I ought to be resentful, I love watching them eat. I love the tremendous mess they make, the way they plow through the food pile as if it could never possibly come to an end. Mostly I love watching them because I know I cannot live like them—no human can, not for long—and this fascinates me.

There is no concept of waste in nature. The name of the game is luxuriant profusion and excess, coupled with luxuriant and precipitous decline. A million moths die in a night; it makes no difference. More will replace them. Yellow jackets live for a season, sustaining the hive to make more yellow jackets; sea turtles lay a multitude of eggs before they hatch; a few lions prey on many gazelles. How much is enough prey? How many of any herd, of any species, needs to be left over in order to re-propagate the species—leaving aside for a moment the question of human intervention? The answer, from nature, is always: there are enough; more will be made; or perhaps more will not be made; there will not be enough; it does not matter.

Nature is neither a capitalist nor a communist economy; there is no such thing as "profit," except in the roughest sense, no such thing as "labor value," and the reinvestment of capital within a species (that is, the species' "excess" propagation of itself) generally occurs even as predators continue to make violent assaults on it, so that an accountant's head would spin trying to take measure of gains and losses. And, though we still like to think of nature as a communitarian enterprise, it is a kind of "community" we can recognize only in sentimental terms. A pride of lions may hunt together, but this pride loyalty does not prevent the male lion from eating his offspring. Nor does any more apparently "private" stake in offspring affect the habits of the male grizzly: he belongs to no pride, but as Thomas McNamee shows, this in no way prevents him from killing and consuming his own cubs. If the matriarchies of lions and grizzlies appear to us somewhat like broken human homes, the analogy works only as far as our sentiment. Male lions and grizzlies are following a species norm, not an exception, in attacking the prey that happens to be their offspring.

I once watched a film on African elephants, in which one elephant, while pushing over a tree to gain access to the higher branches, pushed the tree over on his companion. As the tree fell partway, trapping the other elephant, the first continued to push on the tree trunk, slowly crushing the other elephant to death as it writhed and grunted and gasped. The first elephant was nonchalant; it went on feeding. The death of the other elephant, which it had caused in its search for food, was none of its concern. There was no waste—the death of the elephant was not a waste of the elephant's life in nature; it was just something that happened. There would be more elephants; or not; but what was most important was that the elephant who killed kept on eating.

Speaking in terms of species numbers and in terms of evolution, I am not the norm when I go out to my local garden shop and buy a 25-pound bag of birdseed for $4.99 every 10 days. The finches are the norm. Their wild dispersion and occasional consumption of seed is the norm. What I buy, carefully weighed and valued, with the money I have earned from a job it has taken me years of training and discipline to acquire, they scatter in a few moments' time. And watching them, day after day, I come to see how much human beings are aberrations in nature, the strangers on this planet. We live in strange ways; we judge good and evil; we amass quantities of wealth, not seasonally or simply to keep ourselves and our offspring alive, but for its own sake; we seek security, trying to live as long as we can, looking for meaning beyond the circumstances of our physical existence; we seek love. And not one of these, if one uses the finches as a paradigm of nature, is natural behavior. All of this is aberrant; and the greatest of these aberrations is love.

Thomas Simmons

Among the so-called lower species there is no parallel for love. Anemones do not "love" the rocks they cling to, and ants fighting for their anthill are operating at a programmed level that does not admit to the peculiar varieties and individual explosions of love. Further up the list of species, one begins to run into trouble, or at least a level of anxiety: animals which we commonly eat, such as goats or pigs, are capable of showing loyalty and affection, which many of us read as a kind of love, and even the nuzzlings of a cow, which may or may not be to ease an itch on the nose, can be interpreted as affection such that eating that particular cow causes an ineradicable queasiness. Dogs and cats, the companions that reflect our own species-specific ambivalence about love and possession, demonstrate devotion in very different ways: dogs nuzzle, gather at one's feet, attempt to sit on one's lap, follow one everywhere, show insane enthusiasm for the smallest pleasures, and take pride in obedience training if it is offered them. Cats know devotion is defined by distance: they walk a balance of self-absorption and altruism that drives humans to the point of enslavement. Who cannot love a creature that is always on the verge of leaving? That is the method of the cat. In both these cases, however, humans would insist that cats and dogs are showing love, almost as evolved or complex a love as humans show each other.

Although I have cared for or helped to care for 17 cats and five dogs since I was a child, I don't think that this insistence about love is quite right. Closer to the truth, by contrast, is the gorilla mother (in a televised film on gorillas in the wild) who cradled her dead baby in her arms for three days, setting up a cry so eerily like the human wailing of grief as it echoed through the dense forest that it seemed dangerous to a human soul. If nothing is as complicated as love, nothing is as complicated as talking about love among primates. Yet I know that my current cat adopted us, quite nonchalantly, because he was a stray and had nowhere else to go, and because we fed him. His love, such as it is, is more a matter of loyalty and expectation than anything else, and if we were to move or die he would simply go next door, as he does when we're away for a night, and yowl until our neighbors fed him. He is a survivor, a quintessential natural—rather than aberrant—creature.

And our dog: I bought him for $25 from the dog pound about a year ago as a present for Nathaniel, who had spotted him in a holding kennel and pleaded for him. He was perhaps three or four months old then, an anomalous terrier mix, and may have been separated from his mother quite early. Easily frightened, easily aroused to fierce barking and baring of teeth, slavishly devoted to whomever would pet him, and—this part interests me the most—terrified of food in general and especially if anyone happened to be watching him eat, he was clearly an emotionally crippled animal. He was not a "dog," if dog carries the semiotic meaning I have just described, a kind of half-angel, half-beast put on earth to keep humans company.

Nathaniel named him "Patch," because of the patch of white on his chest; otherwise his coat was a thin, wiry black. He cowered in corners for no apparent reason, shivering when we went over to lift him up and comfort him; around our dinnertime he would explode in fits of snarling, which frightened us briefly until I gathered him up in the middle of one of these and discovered that he would not actually bite, at least not most of the time. After that he no longer frightened Nathaniel or Nathaniel's four-year-old sister Georgia. Still, he tended to prefer plastic and chocolate, both of which could kill him, to any kind of dog food or even people food. After trying several different varieties of dog food, we gave up, allowing him to eat cat food, which he would touch from time to time. We also took to leaving two or three-week-old dog food in his bowl, since he would sometimes crunch down very old food of any kind, as long as he thought no one was looking.

If he found a plastic bag or part of a chocolate bar at some accessible spot in the kitchen, he would devour it; I might come upstairs to find a full-sized plastic bag completely shredded and mostly gone, and Patch with little bits of plastic hanging from his small jowl. Over the past year, although I now buy him a small quantity of raw hamburger each week—the only reasonable food he'll eat—he has lived mostly on whatever cat food, ancient dog food, plastic bags, and chocolate he can scrounge. He has not grown much bigger, and he hasn't died. It is true that he has responded to what we call "love," if that word is read in a limited way to mean the consistent level of comfort, security, and playfulness we provide for him. And he has come to be quite playful, teaching himself—and us—how to throw balls and fetch them, how to chase him when he's got some minor child's toy he shouldn't really have, and how to scratch his stomach while he's chewing on our fingers. Every now and then he will even consent to sit on our laps—a form of animal warmth and security which might or might not be similar to the feeling my children get when they sit on Lesley's lap or mine. At night he curls up on Georgia's or Nathaniel's bed, stretching out lengthwise almost like a person. Yet there is not that dear glow to him that one hears in the stories of true dog lovers. He is, still, a damaged animal; fundamentally, he is simply an animal.

Ironically, perhaps, I feel inadequate around him, as if, for all his strangeness, he were again the norm and I the real stranger. For nothing about him, by animal standards, is particularly peculiar; in nature he would have survived, or not, and my guess is that he would have—did, in fact—survive, gathering his own dog-level neuroses along the way. The two things that drive me craziest about him reflect these neuroses primarily: he needs to escape every now and then, suddenly darting out of the house and disappearing into the neighborhood for an hour or so, wrecking those gardens that don't have fences around them, cavorting with the other, chained-up dogs, and generally inviting our more orderly neighbors to complain bitterly to us once more about our disorderly animals (and children, too, for that matter): and he needs to roll in shit.

Of all the things that Patch does, this is what he does best. He runs over to all the other dogs he can find, and rolls in their shit. When he returns, his coat is filthily matted with other dogs' excrement, matted so badly that he looks like a long piece of shit himself, and he looks exhilarated and disgusted with himself in a way that brings out my ire. He knows that I think he is disgusting, and at some level he seems frightened and confused, but he is not unhappy. The scenario is always the same: after chasing him around the neighborhood for half-an-hour and giving up, I hear him scratching at the door a little less than an hour later. Running into the bathroom to start a bath and to grab a large, old towel, I scoop him up as he cowers by the front door; the stench is enough to make me retch. Before I actually throw up, I get him into the bath, and pour pitchers of water over him as the bath turns brown. He stands meekly before me. Then I lather him up, rinse him, lather him again, and put him down onto the bathroom floor, where he shakes water all over the wall and waits as I rub him down with a clean towel. He is done, then, with roaming, for at least a week, sometimes two, until—without warning—he flies down the stairs where he ordinarily waits at the top, squeaking through a sliver of open space between the door and the door frame as Nathaniel or Georgia goes in or out, and takes off again for another round of dogshit.

Nothing about Patch disgusts me more than this, and yet, clearly, from his point of view, there is nothing "wrong" with it; whatever it is that baffles or confuses him, rolling in shit at least makes him feel happy. Why is it, then, that his happiness revolts me so deeply? It is, of course, because I am human, relatively though not thoroughly normal, and I have been trained in habits of cleanliness and order—more than trained, in fact; I have been raised with a cultural taboo against excrement, so that I could only roll in it if I were temporarily or chronically insane. I have also been raised to appreciate a certain kind of autonomy, which ironically depends a great deal on human love and compassion but depends equally on not doing things that draw great and disgusted attention to me (I put myself at the edge of this prohibition regularly, of course, by being a writer). Watching Patch as he sleeps, knowing that I feel a certain love and pity for him, I realize again that this love is what sets me apart from him, makes me an anomaly in the creation in which he lives, even as he seems to depend on me. His world does not depend on love; whatever bad things, or things that I might consider bad, happened to him before he showed up at the dog pound, he outlasted them. Encoded in his strange genetic mix was an ability to endure situations that would likely have left a higher-order, less-resilient animal, such as a primate or a human, violently deranged.

My world, however, does depend on love. And how strange this is! I know that I love Nathaniel and Georgia, and that this is different from my animalistic desire to protect them—the desire that, for example, makes me walk up to a construction worker half again bigger than I am and threaten him with bodily harm if he ever yells at Nathaniel again for climbing on one of the local dirt piles. I don't simply want them to endure; their presence illuminates my life, much as my private religious faith does, and I can say this even though there are many times when I wish to be alone, childless, spouseless—even, at times, faithless; when I wish love did not involve other human creatures. But of course that is only one kind of love. What do other kinds of love do? Do they heal, console, torture, break up, break down, enlarge, diminish, create, destroy? Of course they do. And what is analogous to that in nature? Only the forces of nature itself—the hurricanes, the typhoons, the sweet sea breezes in the aftermath; and these are mere metaphors, parallels that almost any human would immediately recognize as essentially false.

 I may be plodding along, worn down by debt and argument, uncertain how to proceed, trying to hang on for the sake of my children, being a good animal, and love suddenly will strike in a form and from a direction I never expected. Another person may appear, echoing old needs and desires, offering comfort of a kind I thought had vanished, and I will suddenly be willing to throw over everything, separating from my furious spouse even as she, suddenly, begins to discover dormant talents and directions, following this new lover because nothing, for years, has so closely echoed something in my heart that said, "Feed me!"—even when, for complex and finally untraceable reasons, the love grows pale and reticent, the lover draws away, I draw away, and I am left standing in a no-man's-land of isolation and debt and lovelessness, with far too many people thinking I have lost my mind. Is this "natural"? No.

 Nor is it natural to have been raised, as I was, to believe that love could heal—that love was evidence of the presence of God, and that a consciousness rich in love could help bring something damaged in this world back into harmony with God's perfection. Believing that love could heal, I had to believe from early on that the natural order was not the ultimate order or reality in the universe, and that—as we grew in God's love—we would find our perceptions of the world drawing closer to God's world. The world, in essence, would change before our eyes, though slowly, and nature would become God's nature, which I knew was something quite different. What made it possible for this to happen was that, as the Bible said, God had made us "a little lower than the angels." But if we were a little lower than angels, what were we? Not animals—although we had illusory (as I was taught) animal bodies. We did not fit; we were not part of nature. We were something else.

 Although I have sometimes made much of the way my upbringing was different from other people's, I do think that something endemic in western human consciousness instructs it to know itself apart from nature, as different; and this is not fundamentally a comfortable feeling. It is the feeling of Emily

Thomas Simmons

Dickinson in many of her poems, perhaps most famously in "Further in summer than the birds"; it is the feeling of Herman Melville in the South Pacific, or the tubercular young Yvor Winters in a sanatarium in New Mexico, wondering if he would die. In the American tradition particularly, the consciousness that allows us to meditate on the continent we have come to is also the consciousness that divorces us from creation, that makes the conquest of nature a kind of cynical consolation prize for this divorce, and that fires our rage as we subjugate more and more of the natural world, when one might have thought this subjugation would make us feel more satisfied and peaceful. At the top of the list of things that separate us most from nature is the quality that makes us most human: love.

Is it our fate, then, gradually to leave the natural world behind? Is love the sign of our intermediate nature, a true identifier of human beings as a little below the angels, and if this is so do we ultimately have a quasi-angelic fate? Is the story of the resurrection of Jesus, so commonly doubted these days, really a story about a process of transformation endemic to humans, a divine rather than a cynical consolation for our alienation from earthly soil?

My son Nathaniel is gifted with a talent I find remarkable: he can confer peace on other living creatures, non-human as well as human. He loves animals of all varieties, raises tadpoles at home, catches snakes and butterflies and sets them free, knows the names of bugs I cannot even identify. One of his favorite animals is an enormous Siberian Husky named Roger, whom our neighbors down the street bought in a fit of romanticism because they imagined themselves homesteading in the great north instead of living in a tiny zero-lot-line condominium in Iowa City, and because Roger was an exceptionally cute and small puppy. A year into his life, however, he is enormous. On four legs he is taller than Nathaniel's waist, and when he stands on his hind legs he is a good head taller than I am. He also weighs more than I do. The force of his nudge, even when he is feeling friendly, is enough to knock me off my feet. When he is not feeling friendly, he is a fearsome creature, straining at his chain and howling or tearing apart the occasional muskrats he manages to catch as they come across the lawn of the condominium to or from the wetlands park nearby. Most of the time he is quiet and sad; he lies down, staring, or sleeps. He needs acres to run in, but both his masters work during the day, and he spends eight or more hours of every day of his life at the end of a 15-foot chain.

Does he love Nathaniel? Given what I have already said, he ought not to be able to. Nevertheless, Nathaniel seems to know when Roger is especially sad, and goes over to him, even though this puts him perilously close to a particularly vicious hag of a neighbor who cannot wait to scream at him for any real or imagined infraction of her worldview. And Roger, who may have been howling his weeping howl or may simply have been lying quietly but not restfully for some time, leaps up with joy, bumping against Nathaniel just hard enough to convey affection, not knocking him over, not trying to hurt him or pin him down, just bumping him, making little joyful yelps, and Nathaniel gives Roger a big hug, and caresses his long, silky back over and over.

Roger will stand there, comforted, and then slowly will ease himself down at Nathaniel's feet, so that he half-curls around my boy, who bends down to keep on petting him; and so they are entwined, boy and dog, in what I take unsentimentally to be a kind of benediction—unsentimental because it seems to me rare, not only something I have infrequently done but something I have not often seen, a person and an animal creating a space around themselves as serene as a Buddhist meditation. And then I think: we must take *that* natural world with us when we go, if we rise somewhat like the angels toward a more capacious creation. Perhaps what I witness when I watch Nathaniel and Roger is something actually deeper than love, or something beyond love—the set of instincts or intuitions still in us, which love directs and modifies, but which are creaturely rather than aberrant, and point toward a connectedness we loving human beings too rarely feel.

But this, I must confess, feels to me a little like a trick of language, a way of looking for something other than "love" to call Nathaniel's compassion and Roger's response. When I watch Nathaniel and Roger, I know there is nothing, strictly speaking, "necessary" about their encounter, nothing naturally ordained; yet something is ordained by the fact that they are two creatures on this earth, altering each other's lives slightly, in ways my understanding of moths and bees and turtles and elephants does not quite accommodate. The natural world may be loveless. But what is it when love is present? And what is it when that love is not directed from human to human primarily, but from human to the creation—or rather, is something a human feels as I might imagine myself feeling the heat of the earth's core if I meditated on it long enough, and then directed it outward, as if by instinct, to anyone or anything that came across my path? Love is still the aberration, then, something apart from the normal functioning of things; but it is a beautiful aberration, of the kind that occurs when a certain stranger sits down in a darkened, crowded restaurant, and everyone notices, and an indescribable peace descends.

Thomas Simmons

Ghost Man

How much room does a grizzly bear need to survive? R. Edward Grumbine, citing research by Frank and John Craighead in the early 1970's, observes that a single female grizzly needs about 64,000 acres for a home range. The Craighead studies, as Grumbine and other animal biologists are quick to note, serve as models for estimates of bear populations and bear home ranges in other areas. Jon Almack, for example, estimates that "an average bear [in the North Cascades ecosystem] uses a home range of about 100 square miles," about one-third the size of the average adult male home range in the more arid Greater Yellowstone ecosystem. Looking at the North Cascades ecosystem—an area identified by the Canadian border to the north, Puget Sound to the west, Interstate 90 to the south, and the border of national forest land near the Columbia River valley to the east—one finds an area of about 5.7 million acres of U.S. government property, along with an additional 300,000 acres of state and private land. It's a big chunk of the United States—but not that big by bear standards; animal biologists such as Almack argue that such an area may be enough to sustain about 130 grizzly bears, not enough to ensure their survival in this region.

What intrigues me most about these figures is the element of approximation. These are still rough numbers because bears are hard to find, and because they differ in their need for habitat. Grizzly mothers need the most, but some need less than 64,000 acres; some need more. Adult males generally need less, but it is, in fact, hard to generalize about them: as Grumbine says, "Grizzlies do not limit themselves to ecosystem cores, the North Cascades grizzly bear ecosystem, or international boundaries." The shape as well as the size of home ranges differs; some bears may easily travel more than a hundred miles in a particular direction because that is what they want to do, and the land is there for them to do it. "Averages can be misleading..," writes Thomas McNamee in *The Grizzly Bear*, "especially in so individualistic a species. Those Yellowstone adult male home ranges that average out to three hundred eighteen square miles, for example, may represent many individual bears, one of whom uses one hundred seventy-eight square miles and another of whom seems to need six hundred thirty-three!"

Although home range size estimates are far more than rough guesses—the Craighead Yellowstone study was based on years of careful research, and current research goes so far as to employ satellites to map prime grizzly habitat in its relation to human encroachment—the one thing we know best about grizzlies is that minor but insistent human contact damages them. A dirt road, for example, cut through the wilderness so that loggers may log or geologists may search for oil, imperils bears simply by existing; it marks a foreign boundary that they may rarely if ever cross, thus limiting themselves to far less land than they need to feed themselves, mate, and give birth. According to another researcher, Arnie Dood, 48 percent of all known grizzly fatalities occur within one mile of roads. Bears need enormous quantities of forest and meadow and mountain slope, with no human intrusion or very limited intrusion, in order to survive; but this limited human contact also means that humans are frustrated in their desire to gather the kind of statistics that prove things to people who believe in numbers above all. Bears roam; they are generally secretive; their needs vary. Most of them are, as Grumbine says, "ghost bears."

The same is true for wolves. While wolf packs may identify a specific territory and remain more or less within it—as the three wolves of Ninemile Valley in Montana did in 1991 and 1992, staking out an area of about 110 square miles for themselves—lone wolves, known as "dispersers," may travel much farther. "The farthest overall dispersal," writes Rick Bass in *The Ninemile Wolves*, "is 1500 kilometers (over 829 miles) by a wolf in Canada, an act which, if undertaken by any of the Glacier [National Park] wolves, would put them clearly into the prey-infested woods of Yellowstone." While wolf habitat may show a median figure, there is no "standard" size, and the median graph would be skewed out to the right—out from a center peak of, say, 100 square miles to hundreds of square miles, depending on which lone wolf you were following. All of these animals need lots of space; some need as much space as they can possibly find in their whole lives.

How much room does a human need to survive? I don't think anyone has ever asked me that question, although I've asked it to a number of people over the years. The answers vary widely, but many of them have a domestic ring, as if I were asking, "How many rooms would your ideal home have?" or "Is one-third of an acre enough for a yard, or would one-half be more desirable?" What's most interesting to me about these answers is the implicit dimension of community—not "community" in the abstract or philosophical sense, but a physical connectedness with other human beings through the medium of property. The right amount of space for a human being is whatever you settle into in your chosen part of town.

In Massachusetts, where I lived before moving to Iowa, we rented a two-bedroom flat in what was called there a "triple-decker"—three flats in a tall, barn-like building with a gambrel roof and gables. Our triple-decker was perhaps twelve feet away on either side from other triple-deckers, which were the same number of feet away from other triple-deckers, and so on: it was a triple-decker neighborhood. And this was utterly conventional in that part of Massachusetts, though I had never seen anything like it in California. The families on either side of us had grown up in these buildings; the woman downstairs from us had raised three children in her flat. In fact, much of our neighborhood consisted of retired people who had lived all their lives in these tall, narrow buildings on what seemed to me stubby, narrow lots. For them, the amount of space provided by a two-bedroom flat with one small yard to be shared by three families was just right. Or, if it wasn't right—if they had, secretly and for years, coveted the large, single-family homes a half-mile away on Brattle Street in Cambridge—they rarely mentioned it. They had been car salesmen and heating repairmen and coal deliverymen and housewives, and for them the world had less space, and they knew it.

Although I was grateful to the person who had found us our flat in this neighborhood—rental housing in the Boston area at that time was virtually unfindable—I felt strangled among these triple-deckers. On walks around the block I could feel their narrow tallness looming over me; running or walking, the sense of confinement never changed. Other people who needed minor relief from the neighborhoods sought it in rambles through Mt. Auburn Cemetery, a 10-minute walk away, but the irony of this seemed overwhelming to me: to find room to be human, you had to walk among the dead. I could not do this.

What I began to realize through all of this, however, was that I was becoming a ghost man—not a dead man, or a denizen of cemeteries, but a man who craved a habitat large enough that he could, if necessary, vanish into it. And I began to realize that while many people I knew harbored some fantasies of escape, most of these tended to be thoroughly practical—specific vacations in specific places, retreats in New Hampshire or the Maine islands with friends—and all were rooted in notions of property—airfares to be paid, houses to be rented. There was something, it seemed, odd about my notion of a home range that no one else could find or share without my consent (or could do so only at risk of a major brawl of the kind one finds between territorial animals). What identified me as a ghost man was my need for a home range. For the other people I talked to, it seemed that there was home, and commuting, and work, and vacation havens, and a few other places of special meaning with special resources (parks with state-of-the-art playgrounds, historical buildings, specific vistas), but none of these was really a range, nor was any of it really private. "What can you mean?" a colleague asked at one point when I half-jokingly brought up the subject. "We have jets. We can be in Paris in seven hours. I could be in Nairobi tomorrow. The whole world is our range."

Thus I realized my eccentricity. For it seemed to me that the humans I knew were proud of having the whole world as their range; they had few territorial restrictions, and their hope was to be able to overcome even those over the course of a lifetime. They were not animals; they were citizens of the world. But I was an animal, and what I craved more than anything else in Massachusetts was space. Everything else—love; happiness; security; a sense of selfhood—seemed to emanate from that one goal. And I could find no space in Massachusetts. No matter how far I went into the country, many people had already been there—or were still there. In the most isolated woods I was no more than a few miles from a spot of considerable historical value to humans. When, in summer 1991, I almost crashed an airplane into Mt. Greylock, it interested me in passing to think that I would have first hit, not the mountain, but a monument on top of it erected by humans. In Massachusetts I was a nascent ghost man in a cage.

Even so, it intrigued me to see how various were my neighbors' needs for space. Our downstairs neighbor lived almost exclusively in her five rooms; she went to church on Sundays, and once or twice a year she went to the Cape to visit her grandchildren. Otherwise she stayed at home, though she was by no means physically housebound. Her home range was by and large about 1,000 square feet. The retired Ford salesman and his wife went out somewhat more often, and had a car to drive; their home range seemed anecdotally larger, but what most distinguished them was their move into the back yard during the summer, which expanded the 1,000 square feet of their indoor range by an additional 2,000 square feet or so.

The triple-decker across the street, which had been converted into three condominiums, housed some of the most adventurous people on the block: the people on the ground floor, who became good friends of ours and whose children happily played with our children, planned weekend outings about once a month, and a couple of trips to southern Maine each summer. Their extended families, largely gathered in the Boston area, drew them out of the neighborhood fairly often. And the young man and woman next door to them were avid bicyclists, heading out on nice weekend days in their Lycra tights and beautiful riding shirts and not returning until dark.

Why shouldn't these versions of human space be called home ranges? Perhaps I'm just being cranky about protecting my terminology (as well as something even more earthly than words). And it's true that some fine paradoxes emerge if "range" gets applied to all this human space. Those of my neighbors who stayed home, for example, whose range was most confined spatially, were also those with the most privacy; those who traveled some distance from home did so among smaller or larger crowds of people. Can one be said to have a large "home range" if that range includes the downtown population of Boston on a Saturday afternoon? And how does one measure that range? Does one divide it into percentages, a tiny portion for each person, or does one simply acknowledge that, for most humans, the best home range always includes a large shared component?

The problem, for me, with this notion of sharing is that it diminishes the value of the range in relation to people. It assumes that people are the primary reason for other people to gather somewhere, and that those gathering places become a kind of background to the gathering itself. They may be great backgrounds—in fact, virtually everyone I know would vehemently argue *against* the notion that the Boston Museum of Fine Arts or the Fogg Art Museum at Harvard are "backgrounds" to human gathering—but their purpose is subordinate to the humans who come to them. It begins to seem, then, ironically, that "place" for human beings is at this point something of an abstraction, a concept or category that has more to do with *how* humans interact that with any primary relationship between one person and one place.

True habitat-based animals have none of these problems. Whether or not they think abstractly (and it seems clear that, at the higher end of the evolutionary scale, they do), the home range *is* the place, the home. It is where the animal lives out its most intimate contact with the earth and with those few members of its species it may bring into this world—as mates, as offspring. It is where the animal can avoid contact with all but that which is most precious and necessary to it; it is—and I do not mean this sentimentally—the animal's soul turned outward and invested in the world. This is what I wanted so much in Massachusetts, and what I want equally and have not found in Iowa, where the suburbs spill into the corn fields and success is measured in various terms of domestication.

Of course humans have all along found ways of defining a psychic home range in the midst of excessive human habitation or regulation. Though various historical examples come to mind, what strikes me most powerfully whenever I think of this is the conclusion of Marilynne Robinson's *Housekeeping*. Ruth and her aunt Sylvie, unable to fit into the poor and well-mannered community of Fingerbone, Idaho, set fire to the family house and become transients. They ride the rails; their home range is not a place, but movement.

From such movement comes anonymity and almost infinite choice: Where do we want to go? Who shall we be there, or there? No one will ask about us; decent society will shun us. Thus we will be free to roam. It may be that, from time to time, a railroad watchman will chase us away, or will call the city police or the county sheriff, and we will find ourselves fleeing across fields, too obviously pursued, or stuck for a night or two in jail; but otherwise no one will invade our privacy. And if privacy is what humans sacrifice most in this culture—if we are, more often than we admit, on show for other humans—the life of the transient has at least this distinction: a retreat into a social stature so diminished and frightening to those with property that transience becomes a *de facto* privacy, and may thus count as a home range.

But it is, at least for me, a range with too great a cost. Marilynne Robinson does not romanticize her characters or their lives, and yet there is a quieting of danger and misery in the transience of the two women that finally arouses my suspicion. Would I consider myself to be "home" in a freezing boxcar in the middle of nowhere in the middle of the night, with a drunken man at the other end of the car whose remarkably steady gaze signals a power I do not know how to deflect? To travel this way is always to be, potentially, a victim, whether woman or man. It is fair to say, of course, that there are also "victims" in nature, if one wants to think of them that way; the prey of the predatory may be seen as a victim, although James Dickey's "The Heaven of Animals" suggests why that may not be a true or complete interpretation of predation. To be strong in one's own habitat, however, is not to be a victim; it is to be home. This is the home I seek.

In the fall of 1991, which is now beginning to seem like ancient history, I imagined my home range just east of the North Cascades, in a rundown farmhouse well off the main road, bordering the national park. (A dream of property? Perhaps—but property connected to other *land* rather than to people, and thus unusable as a tool of human community.) There I would live by writing and would run, more or less on the side, a raptor center for injured birds of prey. That may have been a romantic fantasy, but it captured accurately both the geography of my heart and my need for space. I still ask myself: Will I ever get there? Or, once getting there, will I discover that I have deceived myself? Will I find that what I call the "geography of my heart" exists always metaphorically, and that a particular location may be spiritually right but physically wrong? Will I find that I was seeking something, or some place, quite different? I do not know.

But I do know that humans, as creatures of earth and spirit (or of the literal and the abstract), do have a slightly different version of range to draw on. I retreat to that much larger range, for example, whenever I begin to write. And the writing shows me that I am a "disperser," traveling down half-overgrown dirt roads to places I know to be wilderness, in parts of the North Cascades I still have not yet seen, or farther places where the roads end—quadrants of the Yukon or the eastern border of Alaska where the few people who have laid out trap lines or who hunt or fish for subsistence have told few people they are there and do not intend to tell more. It may be that such places will be my literal destination, and I will become the ghost man whose nascent presence within me keeps me pacing the kitchen floor late into the night and writing in the cool of the day.

Until then, my ghostliness is a matter of keeping private something that is precious to me, a neat trick indeed for an autobiographical writer. But the secret of autobiography seems to me to be, at bottom, the art of the secret: it is a matter of writing closer to the heart than most people commonly regard as safe or sane, while knowing that in the heart's finest recesses, beating powerfully, a desire and its realization lie together, beyond words, beyond revelation.

Thomas Simmons

PART II

Rifleman

Thomas Simmons

Rifleman

As time passed, certain images of Crow Pass became more distinct in my mind, but they acquired different meanings from the ones I had originally given them. Again and again, for example, I thought of rifles: everyone had had rifles. And I had dismissed those who were armed as macho or worse, granting my guarded approval only to the two hunters who seemed to me, somehow, truly to belong there. They had earned their weapons, but both they and their high-powered rifles seemed as alien to me as a meteorite. I was unarmed for a reason: I did not, in some abstract sense, believe in killing, but I also saw myself as traveling to Crow Pass in a receptive rather than a defensive mode. I had lost much, and yet still sought something undefinable and fundamental whose roots seemed to lie in this high country. I would take what the country gave me, even if it were death. My human life was less important than the act of being in that place, and thus enacting a dream that had kept me alive months before. There was irony enough in this attitude, but I did not notice it, and only in the passing of time did I begin to feel uncomfortable with my own range of contradictions and my harsh judgments of those who traveled with cartridges in the magazines of their highly-visible rifles and pistols.

But in those first few months away from Alaska, when I fought to keep the trip in the forefront of my imagination, I began to read about bears. There were, as it turned out, good books to read by people who had devoted themselves to researching the habits of black bears and grizzlies—people like Frank and John Craighead, Stephen Herrero, Thomas McNamee. And what they had to say began to bother me. What were the chances of being attacked by a bear in the wild? Not large, as one might expect. During the 1970's, for example, according to Herrero, bear-inflicted injury rates in Glacier National Park, Montana were one injury per 1.3 million visitors; for Yellowstone, the rate was one injury per 1.5 million visitors. On the other hand, bear attacks clearly had something in common with, say, a cooling failure at a nuclear plant: things could get out of control rapidly, and help was not always at hand. Herrero's book *Bear Attacks: Their Causes and Avoidance* was in no way sensationalist; it straightforwardly acknowledged the nature of the danger. While humans were relatively unlikely to come upon bears in the wild, Herrero observed, especially if they made lots of noise and took other precautions in known bear country, the odds of escaping death or a serious mauling declined sharply if a human happened to surprise a bear on or near a trail.

Bear Attacks dispassionately offers survivors' stories of such attacks, as well as reports of attacks in which the victim is killed: Barbara Chapman, for example, a park naturalist, killed and partially eaten in July 1976 in Glacier

National Park, Canada; Dr. Barrie Gilbert, seriously mauled by a grizzly in Yellowstone in June 1977; Judith Donaldson, a wildlife biologist, seriously mauled in the Spatsizi Wilderness Park in northern British Columbia in June 1976; Cynthia Dusel-Bacon, seriously mauled with the loss of portions of both arms in the Yukon-Tanana Upland of Alaska, August 1977; Trevor and Patricia Janz, mauled in Waterton Lakes National Park, Canada, September 1983; Ernest Cohoe, mauled with the loss of most of his face in Glacier National Park, Montana, in August 1980; Brigitta Fredenhagen, pulled from her tent by the neck and partially consumed in Yellowstone National Park, July 1984. And these are samples, of which the book offers many more. "Grizzly bears also kill far fewer people in the United States...than does lightning...or the bites or stings of venomous animals," Herrero writes. Still, if you happen to have a sudden encounter with a grizzly, your chances of surviving unscathed are not good.

It takes a certain kind of outlook, however, to think about these matters. Something had happened to me between the time I left Alaska and the time I began to read about bears. There I knew that I had wanted to lose myself to find myself, and that the experience had a fundamentally spiritual context. Instead, however, I found—well—words more than anything else; I found, back in Iowa, a long stretch of time ahead of me, time to think and to realize that whatever I had hoped to find had not materialized in any way that I could recognize. I was still very much the person I had been months or even years before I went to Alaska. "The expected miracle," as the poet Thom Gunn once wrote, "did not take place."

At first I just spent time staring at the rifles and shotguns for sale in local stores. One of the two wilderness outfitters in Iowa City, Fin & Feather, carried a complete line of .22's, shotguns, and high-powered rifles, along with archery and fishing paraphernalia and the assortment of tents, backpacks, sleeping bags, boots, and other supplies that usually drew me there. I knew absolutely nothing about rifles, but since I was more or less a regular customer, it didn't seem to bother anyone that I'd drift back to the back counter, eyeing various weapons slowly, asking no questions, smiling and saying "no" to the two men behind the counter if they asked if they could help.

While one of the men who worked the gun counter was a classic of the genre—solidly built, gruff, seemingly unapproachable—the other, Larry, was the opposite: affable, humorous, and welcoming. Despite my desire to rationalize my interest in rifles as a way of guaranteeing my return to Alaska—this time, I told myself, I would travel like a seasoned backcountry denizen, trained and prepared for any emergency—I had a feeling that something more profound was pushing me toward guns, and I neither liked nor trusted that impulse. But I liked and trusted Larry. And finally, one day in June 1993, I asked him what he'd carry to Alaska to protect himself against a sudden bear attack at close range.

His eyebrows went up slightly. "Alaska, eh? When you goin'?"

"Maybe August. Went there last summer. They had a couple of bear attacks when I was there, and everyone but me had guns."

"I'm not surprised," he said. "Close-range protection what you want? You're not gonna hunt."

"Nope," I said, a shade too definitely. Turning to the stock of 30 or 40 rifles and shotguns behind him, he reached in one smooth motion for what struck me as a rather short, dangerous-looking weapon with a beautiful black barrel and a polished hardwood stock.

"Remington 870 Express," he said, handing it to me over the counter. I reached for it awkwardly. How much would it weigh? What if I dropped it? I gripped it tightly around the center metal piece just forward of the trigger. It was quite a bit lighter than I thought it would be.

"This is perfect for what you have in mind," Larry said. "It's light, it's easy to carry, it packs a wallop at close range. If you go knocking on doors at farmhouses around here, you'll find most farmers have one of these in the house for personal protection."

I lifted it to my left shoulder—I'm left-handed—and sighted down the barrel. The shotgun felt steady and well-balanced in my hands. Immediately I felt panic and embarrassment: I was aiming a shotgun. I was aiming it indoors. What if someone walked in front of my sights? I felt suddenly unclean, dangerous.

"Ah—how does it, ah, work?" I put the 870 down on the padded counter in front of Larry.

Larry pulled back sharply on the polished wooden handle under the barrel. Kush-UNK—a little cut-out in the metal heart of the gun opened up. I could see into the barrel.

"Pull back on this pump handle here to open the breech," he said as he must have said to people like me for 20 or 30 years. "Then you can drop a shell right in there and—" he kush-UNKed the pump handle forward, and the breech closed again—"you're ready to fire. After firing, you pull back on the handle, the spent shell pops out of the breech, and a new shell pops in if you've got any in the magazine."

He turned the shotgun over to show me an opening in the lower side, covered by a spring-loaded metal tongue. "The 870'll hold four shells in the magazine and one in the chamber—gives you five shots total at a time," he said. "You slide shells into the magazine by pressing them up against this thing here"—he lifted up the black metal tongue—"and pushing them forward. When the rifle ejects the shell, this mechanism lifts a fresh one into firing position. It's real simple."

I picked up the shotgun again and pumped the action, hearing the smooth but oddly loud sound of well-machined metal and watching the breech open and close. I aimed again, at a far wall. Swinging the barrel down to my side, I raised it suddenly and took aim: one-thousand-one. Too slow. A brown bear charging at 30 miles per hour would cover 44 feet a second; it would take less than four seconds to cover 50 yards. To get even two shots off in that time, I would have to be able to aim, fire, and reload in little more than one second. It would have to be instantaneous, second nature, not elegant and careful, as I was here. I felt foolish.

And yet...other kinds of judgments, which I had never made before, swung into my mind. The shotgun would be the most powerful piece of equipment I had never owned. It would be one of the most precise, most durable things I had over owned. It would be very dangerous. It would protect me. It could harm me. I thought suddenly of Merlin, the magician I'd most wanted to be as a child. That desire had never faded. But Merlin had no need for shotguns.

The shotgun, however, was also very sensual. The finish on the black barrel and the heavy metal centerpiece (called the "receiver," as Larry explained) was smooth but not perfectly smooth; it had something of the roughness of heavily suntanned skin. The walnut stock gleamed quietly in the florescent store light, putting to shame the cheap veneers that surrounded me most of the day—cheap veneer bookshelves made of pressboard, cheap veneer window trim and door trim, cheap veneer everywhere. Ironically, in a machine designed to kill, the quality of craft was very high. As I held this shotgun, I knew I was going to do something I had never intended to do.

"I'd like to buy this," I said. Instantly in the pit of my stomach a hard imaginary ball formed, as I knew it would, making me feel sick, and a flash of fever came over me as it always does when I make decisions that go against my own private conservatism. At one time I used to think of this response as my equivalent of Socrates' "No," warning me of a bad decision, but I was not as fortunate as Socrates. My "no's" were not reliable; many of the decisions that caused me such a moment of refusal or revulsion turned out to be crucial changes in my life. And now that I had said a "yes," I could not easily take it back.

Larry put the shotgun back on the rack. "This one's for display," he said. "It'll take about 10 days to get you one. Want to leave a deposit?"

I did; the 870 Express arrived about a week later. As I stood at the counter, filling out the federal firearms transaction form (Was I a fugitive? Had I been convicted of a felony?), I felt much more dangerous than I had ever felt before or ever wanted to feel, and as I walked out of the store, carrying the deep green Remington box, I felt proud and also despised myself, and could not find clear meaning in either response.

II

The Remington Model 870 Express shotgun is 40 1/2 inches long and weighs about 7 1/4 pounds unloaded. It shoots a number of different types of shells—more than I ever knew existed: game loads, heavy game loads, sport loads, steel and lead target loads, heavy dove loads, premier field loads, extra long range shotshells, nitro-mag shotshells, turkey loads, magnum shotshells, premier and express buckshot, rifled slugs, and copper solid sabot slugs. Of these, as it turned out, what interested me most were the cheapest—the game loads and target loads—and the most expensive—the 00 and 000 buckshot and the sabot slugs.

The sabot slug was essentially a very large bullet tucked into the front end of a high-powered shotgun shell. It would stop a very large animal within a hundred-yard range, as long as the shooter had the luck or skill to aim carefully. The buckshot—nine to 15 good-sized nickel-plated pellets stashed inside the shell—were more forgiving: the slight spread of the shot pattern made it less imperative to have perfect aim. On the other hand, the impact of the shot was less than the impact of the sabot slug, raising the odds that a charging grizzly, though mortally wounded, would still have the strength to continue his charge.

The largest sabot slug manufactured by Remington, the three-inch magnum shell, left the muzzle of the rifle at 1,500 feet per second, slowing slightly to 1,307 feet per second at 50 yards and 1,155 feet per second at 100 yards. It did, as Larry suggested, pack an incredible wallop: 2,498 foot-pounds of energy at the muzzle, 1,896 foot-pounds at 50 yards and 1,481 foot-pounds at 100 yards. While the velocity of the sabot slug rivaled none of Remington's hunting ammunition (the 30-06 cartridge, for example, the smallest recommended for bears, left the muzzle at around 2,700 feet per second and was still traveling around 2,485 feet per second at 100 yards), the impact of the slug was roughly in the same ballpark: 1,896 foot-pounds at close range compared favorably with the 30-06's 2,200 or so foot-pounds at 100 yards. Like many people obsessed with sports, gun owners, I learned, can be consumed with statistics, but there seemed to be no point in quibbling about a couple of hundred foot-pounds of impact at short range. The point was, a correctly-aimed sabot slug had the power to stop a bear.

But I had no idea what it would feel like to shoot a sabot slug. When I'd asked Larry what kind of recoil the shotgun had, he smiled a remarkably wan smile and said, "Oh, you'll know it when it hits you—'specially shooting slugs. You might want to start off with some target load first to get used to it." This sounded like good advice, but I was also immediately intrigued with the problem of the slugs. They apparently had a nasty recoil. I was five feet eight inches tall and 125 pounds; what would a "nasty recoil" do? Knock me over? Break my shoulder blade? These seemed like extreme possibilities, but I had never shot a shotgun before, and no one seemed able to give me much idea of what it would feel like. Undeterred, I bought a box of 20 target shells ($4.99) and a box of five sabot slugs (the same price) and headed for the local rifle and pistol range in West Liberty.

About 14 miles southeast of Iowa City, West Liberty gives every appearance of being a model midwestern town. Its success centers on farming, local

Thomas Simmons

business, and a Louis Rich turkey processing plant just across the tracks from the Chevrolet dealership and the rest of the downtown commercial district. Its small population of semi-indigenous Iowans is augmented by a smaller contingent of semi-transient University of Iowa professors and staff members looking for cheaper housing and a larger contingent of Chicanos, many of whom work in the turkey plant and have put down serious roots in the community. I had been through the town several times: once in 1992 to see if I could find an affordable place to live (I couldn't—even in Iowa my debt was too large, my salary too small), and later to test-drive my 1981 Subaru after repairing it or to try to lull my daughter Georgia to sleep after a fitful afternoon or evening. There was a deep peacefulness to the houses lining the side streets, and the one movie house downtown showed second-run films for two bucks. It was a town to like. I had never, however, driven past the turkey processing plant, and I had to do that now in order to get to the West Liberty Gun Club on West Prairie Avenue.

The plant itself looked anonymous and comfortingly industrial, as most well-run plants do; it might have been a huge, air-conditioned warehouse for perishables of one kind or another.

Across the street from the plant, however, was a tall, sideless shed—perhaps 14 or 15 feet tall—with huge fans attached to the poles supporting the roof. And beside those huge fans stood three or four trailers filled with live turkeys.

For anyone who has never been close to a meat-processing plant, it is strange actually to be confronted with what goes on, or what must go on. For these were not the turkeys one sees in Thanksgiving illustrations, or on farms where they run around gobbling and otherwise looking picturesque. These birds—in wire cages, stacked six high, the whole length of the flatbed trucks—were silent. Their wings were clipped; their beaks were clipped. Their feet were clipped. They did not move; they made no sound. At first, in fact, not really knowing what the plant was, I did not quite know what I was seeing. I thought they might be tightly-bundled packages of down, waiting to be made into something interesting in a plant whose management had thoughtfully air-conditioned it for the sake of the workers. But that didn't seem right. I slowed down; I stopped. There was no other traffic on this narrow road. I stared at what was in the cages. I saw those creatures blink. They were no longer creatures but things to be watered and cooled; they would soon be dead. The only problem was that they were *not* things, and they were *not* dead. And because I was not fully a vegetarian, I would soon be eating such animals as these, half-pruned and robbed of motion and sound, staring, blinking.

Suddenly, full of disgust, I floored the car. I wanted to be away from this place of mechanized death. And in that moment I had what struck me later as a peculiar reaction: I applauded the hunters I had seen in Alaska. I applauded any hunter who hunted for need. Suddenly hunting made perfect sense. It dignified the animals in a way that the soon-to-be-slaughter of turkeys I had just passed could never do. Despite a hunter's overwhelming advantage with his or her high-powered rifle, the hunt was still exactly that: a quest for something elemental, for sustenance, with an uncertain outcome. The hunter had to ask the earth to feed him and his family by successfully tracking and killing his prey; the prey had to sense the threat and flee or die. Predator and prey each mattered as individual beings. To eat meat in this way was to honor animals; to eat them as they are usually eaten in modern America was to dishonor, to desecrate them. Of course it was impossible to imagine 180 million adult Americans hunting their food, and yet the difference still struck me as true. I had never thought of such a thing before. It was unnerving.

And then, quickly, I was driving along the rutted dirt driveway into the gun club, checking in with the range officer, paying my five-dollar user's fee, explaining that I had never shot a gun before as the officer listened and, with a slightly supercilious expertness, took over my instruction. We went to a shed, picked out a target on two wooden stakes, waited for the other gunners on the range to stop shooting, stuck the target into the ground 25 yards out, and came back to the shooters' bench.

The shooters' bench was exactly that: a long bench with 14 positions where shooters could shoot pistols, shotguns, or high-powered rifles. Only three other people were using the range that afternoon. One had a muzzle-loader, a replica of a Revolutionary War rifle; it made a roar so deafening when he fired it that my ears rang for several minutes afterwards. Another, with a high-powered rifle and scope, was using the bench as a rest or brace for the gun, his target 100 yards away. Another man, younger than the rest—barely out of his teens, I thought—was firing a semi-automatic nine-millimeter pistol and a medium-caliber revolver. Both looked like police weapons.

The range officer helpfully went through the loading procedure with me as I prepared the shotgun for firing (he also reminded me to put in my earplugs to protect against the noise). I pulled back the pump handle, watching out of the corner of my eye as a shell went into the chamber and the breech closed over it. I clicked the safety off with my left hand. The shotgun was now ready to fire. All I had to do was pull the trigger, and a wad of target load would leave the muzzle at over 1,000 feet per second. Just like that. Instant death for the target.

I lowered the shotgun slowly to waist level, looking at the target again. With my earplugs in, the sound of the nine-millimeter next to me was more of an oceany, dull roar, like the sound of a fetal heart through a heart monitor. When I raised the gun again to my shoulder, I tried to do it quickly and smoothly, as if I had no doubts. Sighting down the barrel of the shotgun, focusing my eye on the far gunsight, I held my breath and pulled the trigger.

The noise was what made me flinch, despite my earplugs—a heavy thud that went along with the sensation of being punched hard in the left shoulder. It hurt; I was surprised. The sensation was overwhelmingly physical. My ears felt vaguely hollow; I smelled the harsh powder from the shell, an acrid odor I hadn't anticipated; my shoulder ached. It was as if I'd been shot by a very powerful, very precisely-aimed burst from a wind tunnel.

Pulling back on the pump, I ejected the spent shell from the chamber and loaded a new one. I fired again. And again. After five shots, I could feel the bruise developing on my left arm and shoulder, and my body felt tired. The other shooters, I noticed, were also taking a break. Out of the corner of my eye I could see the range officer motioning for us to put down our weapons.

Suddenly a dense quiet came over the place. The other shooters sauntered out to their targets, one of which was a good hike away; the atmosphere changed almost to that of a company picnic. All sense of urgency evaporated. This was clearly a world in which change came swiftly, and I was unprepared for its rhythms. Like the others, I walked out to my target, a mere 75 feet away (to approximate the distance of a charging grizzly) and stared at it. It seemed to be covered with tiny holes; had it been that way before I started shooting? Although someone had previously used this target, I hadn't bothered to inspect it closely. I simply assumed that my target load would leave huge holes in it.

The range officer wandered over. "Well, at least you hit it," he said, grinning. I grinned back, unsure of what to say. It wasn't until a couple of days later, discussing the experience with my gun-loving older brother (who also happened to be, somewhat intriguingly, a professor of religious studies), that I realized the range officer had been teasing me. "Of *course* you hit the target," my brother said, laughing. "At 25 yards, with target load, you could hardly have missed. Do you know what kind of dispersion pattern target load has? You could have aimed deliberately left or right of the target and still hit it dead center."

I returned two weeks later, after my large bruises had shrunk to something seemingly minor. This time I planned to fire the five sabot slugs as well as 15 or 20 target loads. The range was crowded that day; almost all the bench sites were taken. After firing a few rounds of target load, feeling the pain in my shoulder return, I shifted to the slugs: I rang off the five of them in quick succession. Because the previous recoils had dulled the nerves in my shoulder, I didn't notice much difference between the slugs and the target loads. But when I was done, a few seconds later, I realized that several people at the firing bench were staring at me. One of them wandered over.

"What the hell you shootin'?" he asked.

"Sabot slugs," I said, not knowing if I should explain about Alaska, and bears, and having less than four seconds to fire.

"Thought it musta been somethin' special," he said. "Those things sure make a hell of a noise."

I hadn't even noticed.

III

When I was four or five, I had the chicken pox, and I was sick for a long time. No other kids could play with me (not that many did regularly—it wasn't a kid-filled neighborhood), and I spent a lot of time lying around, not doing much of anything. The prayers of my mother and her Christian Science practitioner didn't seem to make a great deal of difference. What I lived for was a TV show starring Chuck Connors, *The Rifleman*, which came on in the early evening. The opening was thrilling: five or six shots fired in quick succession from a Winchester lever-action rifle, and then a long pan up the barrel of the rifle, up the arm of the man with the rifle, to the face of the man, Connors himself—serious, brooding, wounded, angry, determined. I knew all this about him when I saw him. He was a man. And seeing him made me feel better.

After a couple of weeks had gone by and I wasn't much better, my mother came home from the store one day with a present. It was a big present, by my standards: a sheriff's outfit, complete with hat and badge. But what dazzled me was the rifle—a Winchester Model 94, lever-action. It was Chuck Connors' rifle. I carried it with me all around the house for several days, ate with it, slept with it, even sat out on the front porch with it, rocking in the rocking chair and waiting for desperadoes to cross my gunsights. After that, I got better quickly.

Was the toy rifle part of the Christian Science healing? A ludicrous question, I suppose; but my mother had noticed the one thing that made me feel strong at the time, and had found a way of giving it to me. With a Winchester Model 94, I could be a rifleman. I could be a tough guy with a heart of gold, an outcast who did good deeds. I could be high and lonesome, singing a song to myself as I rode through canyons on my favorite mustang. I was dangerous; I knew living and dying. I was serious.

Was I a killer? Sometimes; but only of evil men. I killed them because they had hurt people I knew. They had burned their houses and killed their livestock, terrified them, kidnapped them, treated them as something less than human. With a rifle, I was very human. And this was interesting, because without the rifle I was not human. When I was well, I was more than human—a spiritual idea, a Christian Scientist; when I was sick, I was less than human—a creature mired in an erroneous belief in the mortal body, in the "claim" (as Christian Scientists said) of sin, disease, and death. The sicker I was, the more I was an illusion. Though this was not quite what Christian Science meant to teach me, it was what came through in Sunday School, and so I was always see-sawing between illusion and spiritual idea. Only with a rifle was I human.

It was an incredible luxury to be human—so great a luxury, in fact, that I figured out ways on my own to remain human, at least part of the time, in the years of my childhood that followed. Some of these methods were complicated and, in retrospect, too innocent and too sad; others were failures. But the

Winchester was one of the purest moments of humanity in my childhood, and the one that stayed most clearly in mind through all the intervening years.

The most famous Model 94 was the 30-30, a rifle capable of killing anything from a rabbit or woodchuck up to a deer—or a human. It was not, however, powerful enough to bring down a bear except with a shot right between the eyes. Thus, 32 years after I first held a toy Winchester in my hands, I reluctantly abandoned the idea of owning a Winchester for protection against bears.

But the U.S. Repeating Arms Company, makers of the Winchester rifle, had something on the order of an afficionado's secret that I didn't know about until I checked back with Larry at Fin & Feather. Although virtually all Model 94's were either .22's or 30-30's, two were not—a 307 caliber and one even larger, a 356. The 356, I knew from reading the ballistics catalogues, was a serious high-powered weapon, somewhere between the 30-06 and the 375 magnum. A bullet fired from the 356 left the muzzle at 2460 feet per second, and slowed only a little—to 2,114 feet per second—at 100 yards; its impact at 100 yards was 1,985 foot-pounds. If I was considering getting into a tight corner with a very large animal, the 356 Model 94 would do what no other lever-action Winchester could do: kill it.

It was a strange thing, for a couple of weeks, to roll the purchase of a 356 Model 94 over in my mind. For what I needed, the Remington shotgun would perform perfectly well. It was also enormously cheaper to use than the Winchester. Twenty 356 Winchester cartridges cost almost thirty dollars, as opposed to five dollars for the shotgun shells. In just a few minutes I could shoot through sixty dollars' worth of Winchester ammunition—if I could afford to buy sixty dollars' worth in the first place. It was really a ridiculous sum to spend on bullets.

More important, though, was the implication of buying the Winchester. It could not be what the toy had been for me so many years before—a confirmation of my humanity, my private worth. If I lacked confidence in those qualities now, I was in more difficulty than any rifle could rescue me from, and fantasizing about rescue with a rifle was clearly a dangerous business. And yet, as I thought about that small boy with his rifle, trying to recover from a prolonged illness and utterly unsure of his place beyond the imaginary frontier world of a rifleman, I realized that I wanted to meet him again. He had been gone a long time—pushed aside, overwhelmed by adulthood, brooded and angered almost out of existence. It seemed strange to me that he was a boy who had, for a brief while, seemed to know so much about being a man. I found myself wishing that I knew as much now about manhood as he did at the age of five, watching Connors and believing that he could be alone and good and loved, if only at a distance.

But to think of the real rifle even remotely in the same context as the toy, to think of the man even remotely in the same context as the boy...it was a sentimental fantasy. To own a real Winchester would be to say good-bye to the boy rather than to embrace him. It would be to admit that whatever I knew about being a man, with all its gaps and confusions, was after all simply what I knew; I had no preturnatural child's knowledge of manhood, nor was I particularly good or bad at being a man, despite my furies and frustrations over my own ability to love and to know who I was. Still, there was something about that child with his ironic emblem of humanity, a rifle, and I could not resist the power of that emblem. When I placed the order for the Winchester Model 94 in the 356 caliber, I left the store with a strange feeling of pleasure and calm, as if I were calling back something to which I had never given a name.

In the back of my mind, whenever I thought about guns and children, was the other reality of guns in America—the reality of violence and death, of gang killings of kids in the urban slums and on the city streets and even in the schools of supposedly safe places like Littleton, Colorado and Springfield, Oregon, suburban or semi-rural communities ostensibly removed from hard-core violence. What crystallized this particular horror in my mind was Erik Larson's "The Story of a Gun" in the January 1993 *Atlantic*. Larson explored the saga of Nicholas Elliot, a sixteen-year-old student at Atlantic Shores Christian School in Virginia Beach, Virginia. On December 16, 1988, Elliot walked in with a semi-automatic Cobray machine gun, killed one teacher and wounded another, and then turned to open fire on a roomful of his classmates. Only the desperate intervention of another teacher, who tackled and subdued him, prevented many more deaths and injuries.

It was, as Larson observes, incredible what was available to Elliot: "This guy was ready for war," said the police detective investigating the case. The gun itself, an assault pistol that Elliot easily concealed in his backpack, was a killing machine: Elliot had outfitted it with 32-round magazines—six in all—for a total capacity of 192 bullets. He taped the magazines, the "clips," together in such a way that when one was empty, he could pull it out and ram in the next with exceptional speed. He had fashioned a serviceable silencer from a fabric-wrapped pipe. He had attached a submachine-gun style sling to make the small Cobray more manageable.

Of course, it's easy to rationalize the difference between a semi-automatic assault pistol and a shotgun—or a Winchester. But it's not so easy to rationalize what people do with their weapons. I did not know that, even as I pondered the Nicholas Elliot story, a teenager in Grayson, Kentucky had (in January 1993) killed two classmates with a gun, and another teenager in Amityville, New York had (in February 1993) killed one; nor could I know that, from October 1995 to April 1998, nine different children or teenagers would shoot to death a total of 23 students and one teacher with pistols or rifles. And all of this was before the Columbine High School massacre in Littleton, Colorado—April 20, 1999—the watershed that would change everything.

Thomas Simmons

In 1991—the latest year for which figures were available when I was considering the Winchester 356—38, 317 people were killed by guns; there were 250, 000 injuries. Of the fatalities, 51% were murders, 44% were suicides, and 4% were accidents. Only 1% were self-defense shootings—the kind most often held up as the justification for gun ownership in this country. "Over the past two years," writes Larson in his 1993 article (though his sources are a little unclear if, like me, he had to rely on statistics available only through 1991), "firearms have killed 60, 000 Americans, more than the number killed in the Vietnam War. Handguns account for 22, 000 deaths a year." A few years later, in 1995, the National Safety Council (reporting in 1997) would list 35, 673 people dead from shootings. Interestingly, the statistics flipflopped somewhat: suicides led the 1995 list at 52%, with homicides following (44%) and 3% "unintentional"; the National Safety Council did not report whether the remaining 1% in fact reflected "self-defense shootings."

By 1998, in response to these figures, some newspapers in America (including the *Iowa City Press-Citizen*) were calling guns a "public health problem" rather than a problem of violence *per se*, since the link between guns and suicide starkly raised the question of health and well-being. The National Safety Council noted that gun-related deaths increased 16% between 1986 and 1993, but then began to decline; *Time* took a slightly different benchmark for the decline after the Jonesboro, Arkansas school killings in 1999, noting that "juvenile violence involving guns has actually been in decline since 1994." Nevertheless, deaths numbering in the thirty thousands annually are a lot of deaths; deaths of any kind on a school campus—because, perhaps, of our admittedly naïve notions that schools are still somehow a refuge from the world—remain particularly horrifying.

Among those 38,317 people shot to death in 1991 were six people I first read about while sitting at my dining room table in my apartment in Medford, Massachusetts on Saturday, November 2nd, 1991. It was the week I had separated from my wife and moved to a new apartment; it was the week a storm blew through that, as one weather forecaster said, made the recent Hurricane Bob look like a pussycat (years later, that November hurricane would be immortalized in *The Perfect Storm*). Houses along the coast south of Boston had been washed away; November 2nd was a grim, blustery aftermath. Opening the *Boston Globe* to page three, I found a story about almost equally grim weather in Iowa—and a photograph of someone lying on an ambulance gurney in a snowfall in Iowa City. Since I was scheduled to move to Iowa City in June to take up a new job, I read with curiosity. But now I found Iowa City connected with death: Dwight Nichelson, chair of the department of physics and astronomy; Christoph Goetz, a distingushed professor of physics and astronomy; Robert Smith, a rising star in the department; Linhua Shan, a doctoral candidate in physics; and T. Anne Cleary, associate vice president for academic affairs.

The story had a surreal familiarity. A doctoral student from Beijing, Gang Lu, felt he had been unfairly slighted in the department and was furious that a particular award had gone to the man he considered his rival, Linhua Shan. Having purchased a nine-millimeter pistol the previous May, he practiced until he became proficient in its use, then opened fire on his colleagues as they gathered for a meeting on the afternoon of November 1st. After killing four of them in Van Allen Hall, he crossed the campus to the office of the vice-president, where he fired on Miya Rodolfo-Sioson, a 23-year-old temporary staff member who got in his way; he then killed Cleary. A few minutes later, one floor up, he turned the pistol on himself and committed suicide. Rodolfo-Sioson, the only survivor of the attack, was paralyzed for life.

The numbness that came over me as I read this story—a story about people like me, who had come to Iowa with varying degrees of hope and expectation and distinction, who saw it as a safe and sane place in which to do their work—was at once overwhelming and less than it might have been. I was already numb; whatever rebirth I myself had recently sought seemed stillborn. I was scarcely alive myself to respond. But I came to life several days later when I received a letter from a senior professor in the English department, a woman I had met only briefly during my job interview at Iowa. For those who worked at the University of Iowa, she explained, these killings had changed it forever; it was important for her to tell me that. Her distraught and eloquent letter to someone she hardly knew was profoundly moving, and yet I knew that "profoundly moving" was not her goal. Hers was the anguish of one who desperately wanted to set time back, to have returned what could not be returned. And a gun had done this. A gun had made this enduring misery possible.

All of this was on my mind as I waited for the Winchester rifle to arrive. Whatever explanation I might try to make, I had crossed a certain cultural line when I bought the shotgun. Though any human being who can wield a knife or swing a baseball bat can kill, those who buy guns imply something special about killing—and survival. Life becomes more elemental with a gun in the house, but culture—the culture in which we live—is not supposed to be about elemental things. It is supposed to be about refinements: motions of the logical and reasoning mind; aesthetic judgments; beauty and truth. To buy a gun is to say what no one really wants to say, which is that the foundations of culture are not solid but permeable, and that what permeates them most quickly is any serious encounter with an elemental issue: faith; race; wealth; pride; food; sex; survival. Although I had bought a shotgun, and now a rifle, with a much different notion of survival in mind—a notion that took me out of culture, into the wild, and assumed my inherent weakness in the face of certain animals—my guns also occupied a place within my culture, and spoke a crude and direct language I could neither mute nor modify.

As I thought about this, I realized sadly that this was not so different from other moments of my life—only more emphatic, and wider in its cultural context. If, as a Christian Scientist, I might have been perceived as an eccentric, I was now, as a gun owner, culturally dangerous. Yet my separateness from other people was scarcely different in the two circumstances. For more years than I knew, my quest had been, not for a common language, but for a basic language of survival. This left me somewhere in a wilderness of my own making, a place I could not easily recognize or map. But I knew intuitively, as I waited for the Winchester to arrive, that it was a wilderness of meaning, a place of love and power, not of fear and trembling. I could find a purposefulness within it, even if I could not clearly speak of this to other people. For it was clear that one needed a great deal of self-trust to own a rifle; one had to be certain of one's strength to resist the greatest fears of those for whom guns equal death. And because my trust wavered, I went back to the animal whose ghostly presence spawned my interest in survival, and I began to sense in him the presence of a spirit animal.

IV

In many native American traditions, animals are human guardians, companions, even (what Anglos might call) alter egos, as well as tricksters and harbingers of evil. Their presence in the world confirms our connection with a larger spirit. They may be opponents or prey; yet even as prey they may embody something central in one's own being. Kenneth Fields speaks of this phenomenon in "Trout Watching":

> It has been here before, at every hour,
> Watching the water where I wait. Its head
> Surrounded by soft clouds, and at its back
> Are points of aspen breaking, like the suns.
> The fine straight nose, the light hair, and the fine
> Pale eyes, it knows my vigils. Like a god,
> It is my spirit animal, its wrist
> Flashing, mimicking ripples, floating insects
> Toward me as I rise up. Suddenly
> It gives me fire in this freezing river,
> Where we shall meet forever, at this edge
> Our warmth resisting the insistent pull.

Who is speaking this poem? The trout is speaking; the trout identifies the angler with the "fine straight nose" and "light hair" as its own "spirit animal." Although this may seem a kind of literary trickery, it is fundamentally serious. Too often, Fields implies, white writers return to native traditions without trying to shift away from their own cultural constraints; thus nature is always "object" to them, though perhaps revered object, and the quest is to unlock the secrets of that life outside oneself. But "Trout Watching" suggests precisely the kind of interpenetration of humankind and nature that underlies native traditions, and which is somewhat alien even to the language of English. The trout may not only be spirit animal to the man; the man may be, must be, spirit animal to the trout. There is a playfulness in Fields' poem—the numerous puns in the two-word title, the delight of the fish—but something more, too. All animals on earth invest each other with their being, and to assume that humans alone seek intimate connections with natural forces is to assume a tragic rent in the fabric of creation.

I have assumed that rent, of course, for most of my life. And I am scarcely alone. In their various ways, Bill McKibben and Carolyn Merchant, for example, lament the same tragedy in the contemporary world, while Emily Dickinson speaks of the same sense of rending from a voice unmuted in the passage of more than a century. But there may be—Fields suggests in this poem, and in others—a way beyond that tragedy. It requires an act of the imagination; it requires faith that the imagination is not something apart from nature, a purely human construct, but intuitively related to nature and full of strength at precisely the moment it most clearly imagines the human and the natural springing from a single source.

It is nature that attacks, and nature that redeems, according to Kiowa storytelling. As N. Scott Momaday writes,

> Eight children were at play, seven sisters and their brother. Suddenly the boy was struck dumb; he trembled and began to run upon his hands and feet. His fingers became claws, and his body was covered with fur. Directly there was a bear where the boy had been. The sisters were terrified; they ran, and the bear after them. They came to the stump of a great tree, and the tree spoke to them. It bade them climb upon it, and as they did so it began to rise into the air. The bear came to kill them, but they were just beyond its reach. It reared against the tree and scored the bark all around with its claws. The seven sisters were borne into the sky, and they became the stars of the Big Dipper.

The "tree" is Devil's Tower in northeastern Wyoming—"Tsoai," "Rock-tree," in Kiowa. Momaday's Kiowa name is "Tsoai-Talee," "Rock-tree boy"; his primal connection is to this place, this geologic formation, and this story. Moreover, he points out that from the time of the formation of this story, "The Kiowas have kins[women] in the night sky." The bear attacks the daughters of the tribe, and the tree saves them. They, in turn, watch over their descendents from the realm of nature beyond the earth. It is a theophany in which animals play a revered part, but the reverence does not preclude danger or death. The spirit animals of a tribe are not preserved from harmdoing or even, necessarily, from death. But in their encounters with these animals, the tribe grows in imagination, which is to grow in a sense of one's own value and strength. For humans, the spirit animal is the medium of growth; perhaps the same is true for animals of their own spirit animals.

"The 'guardian spirit complex' is a term which refers to the conceptions and rituals pertaining to the personal guardian spirits which are acquired through visions," writes Ake Hultkrantz in *The Religions of the American Indians*. "Consequently they are not given at the birth of the individual but must (at least in the majority of cases) be sought in secluded places, where they appear in visions to the fasting suppliant. They appear in animal guise but are seldom if ever identical to the animal whose shape they have assumed." It is not possible, then, to choose arbitrarily one's spirit animal as one might choose a pet—because one likes the color of the hair or the look of the eyes, or because of some yearning for a particular animal (although this yearning comes closer to this phenomenon). On the contrary, it is the animal who chooses the "suppliant"; the animal appears at a time of duress in the human's life, when the human signals his or her need through a vision quest. Furthermore, the spirit animal is not fully identified with the physical animal; the physical animal may still be hunted, may still be prey, although it must be treated with particular reverence. The spirit animal, however, can never be hunted; it is always near. It can be driven away, as Hultkrantz writes, only if the human "transgresses any taboo assigned by [the animal]."

Were I to shoot a grizzly bear, then, to save my life as it charged me, I would not be violating a compact with a spirit animal. But this reassurance is riddled with assumptions on my part. Under what circumstances would a bear charge me, if it were my spirit animal? The connection between the spirit animal and the creature in nature is inexact but powerful; why, then, should I even feel concern? Even more to the point, however, is the larger question: why would I think that I, an anglo male, had any necessary connection to spirit animals? Am I a spiritual fraud?

Years ago, when I studied with N. Scott Momaday, he quoted in class a favorite passage from the critic Irvin Howe: "Any graduate student can deal with symbols," he said, "but it takes a first-rate intelligence to deal with the surfaces of literature." The same was true for life, Momaday added: we missed the essential value if we went directly for symbolic meaning (in an age of post-structural semiotics, when everything has a symbolic value that is also, in a sense, a surface value, even less can be learned about the nature of meaning and the nature of surfaces, and much of the power of story is lost). Momaday's invitation was one of the first I had ever had to look at the world *as* world—as a continual stream of phenomena; I could not live in it until I could see it. And since I had spent most of my childhood not seeing it, denying its reality, I had a great deal of blindness to make up for. I have by no means made up for it yet.

It was the bear, or ghost bear, who shadowed my thought and my night at Crow Pass, who shadowed my childhood as well—and who appeared, nevertheless, as a kind of blessed absolute in that Alaskan wilderness, reinforcing my unanticipated difference from other humans on the trail—my willingness, in short, to die. In that willingness I inhabited the bear's world, not the humans' world. Had I carried a rifle, by contrast, I would have declared my allegiance to the human world rather than to the bear world. And it was the bear world that called me most passionately. But it was the human world, whose surfaces I had so rarely seen as a child, that called me with the tone of a spurned lover, pointing out all that I might have missed in my quest for spiritual depth. There was a human life more beautiful than any I had yet seen, it said to me; why should I be in such a hurry to relinquish it? And so I felt a pull both toward the bear, and toward those people who brought rifles to protect themselves from attack. I was not a fraud, I thought, but I was midway on a journey whose resolution could hardly have been more unclear.

Back to the surfaces, back to the surfaces. In a way, this is very much like saying what I said to myself two years ago at Crow Pass: "Who are you, and what do you love?" One can go too deep in search of answers for those questions; sometimes the surfaces are much clearer. This is my surface: I went to Alaska; I was unarmed; the armed humans passed by me and moved far down the trail; I was alone. But in my aloneness I felt a closeness to something animal and something stellar, as if I were both brother and sisters in the Kiowa legend. At some point, given such a surface, one must simply trust—or die.

In *Coming into the Country*, John McPhee quotes Andy Russell, a former hunter of grizzlies who switched to photography, on the relationship between armed humans and bears. "Reviewing our experiences," Russell writes, "we had become more and more convinced that carrying arms was not only unnecessary in most grizzly country but was certainly no good for the desired atmosphere and proper protocol in obtaining good film records." It was better to go unarmed, this expert tracker reported; "The mere fact of having a gun within reach, cached somewhere in a pack or a hidden holster, causes a man to act with unconscious arrogance and thus maybe to smell different or to transmit some kind of signal objectionable to bears...He, being wilder than they, whether he likes to admit it or not, is instantly under even more suspicion that he would encounter if unarmed."

"To smell different or to transmit some kind of signal"? The language worries me, distantly echoing the language of my childhood religion, in which the unreal mortal mind, unregulated by the perfect divine Mind, could on its own disseminate something like "an objectionable signal" in the guise of "sin, disease, and death." This sending of "objectionable signals," known in my religion as "mental malpractice," might wreak harm on ourselves or on others. Because, as a child, I was always implicitly blamed for this kind of thinking—and because being blamed for what was not within my control finally became horrific and intolerable to me—I bridle at the imprecision and the disturbing epistemological implications of McPhee's reporting of Russell's words. And yet I understand the creaturely desire for distance, the soul's wariness of arrogance, and I know how inarticulate and passionate—how animalistic—those feelings can be. Russell, through McPhee, speaks in an impressionistic language, but his observations come from the surface and cannot be discounted, even though one can set against them the encounters between humans and bears—as described in Herrero's book, for example, or John Haines'—in which the bear draws near, and the rifle is the weapon of last resort.

Perhaps more daunting is Russell's vision of the wildness of humans. For Russell, by implication, it is the humans who live in a wilderness, and bears who live in nature. Nature is deadly, but the human wilderness is deadlier; it is the humans who band together for massive good and massive evil, who create cities and wars, who risk consuming the planet with their invented needs, who kill and heal and kill. If, long ago, a toy Winchester rifle made me feel more human, it also made me feel far wilder than I realized. And I have now reached the apotheosis of that wildness: I look upon nature and fear it, wish to protect myself from it, seek to destroy it if necessary, even as I voice a hope to live in consonance with it.

V

To be human is, I think, to desire both something and its opposite or complement. It is to desire nature and society; it is to desire more than one lover, or more than one kind of love; it is to desire companionship and solitude; it is to desire refined intellect and raw intuition; it is, finally, to desire death and life. Over and over again, our place in the natural order of things is confirmed by the fact that only rarely can we have these dualities or complements; our capacity for synthesis is tragically limited. We must choose. Ultimately we must choose death. And it seems that not until then does life magnify itself to us.

It is mid-October, 1993. The Winchester Model 94 has just arrived, and it is beautiful. Larry and I both stare at it for a moment as it sits on the protective pad on the glass counter at Fin & Feather. Its polished walnut stock and black chrome molybdenum steel barrel gleam extravagantly in the florescent light. I pick it up. It's light, only 6 1/2 pounds, and short, a mere 37 3/4 inches, but it's exceptionally well-balanced. My right hand knows just where to grip it, cradling it just ahead of the receiver; the barrel rocks gently down, as it would if I were holding it this way while hiking. When, in a swift move, I bring it up to my left shoulder, my left hand reaches for the lever action as if it had always known just how far to move, how much force to apply. The rifle is now cocked. Were it loaded, I would be ready to fire.

Larry smiles a specific kind of smile—the kind that acknowledges a customer's pleasure in craft. I put the Winchester back down on the counter and begin filling out another federal firearms transaction form. Another customer, a long-time hunter and F & F patron, slides up the counter to check us out. Though he doesn't say anything, I can see he's eyeing the Winchester carefully. "That's not a 30-30," he finally says, more to Larry than to me.

"356," says Larry.

The man lets out a low whistle as if he were on a movie set. "Well son," he says to me, "You got yourself one hell of a Missouri deer rifle."

"More than that, I hope," I say cryptically. Larry understands. In fact, Larry understands a good deal more than I expected. A couple of days ago, when I was in just to look around, I overheard Larry talking with a couple of hunters. It was prime deer-hunting season, and the two men were asking Larry what he'd bagged so far. He let loose a slow smile.

"Well, you know, I've *seen* a bunch of 'em, but until I saw something really special I just couldn't bring myself to shoot. Been filming a lot of 'em, though."

There was a brief pause. "Beg pardon?" one of the men said.

"Video," Larry said. "Been taking a lot of video."

The conversation changed to another subject. But I'd been thinking about Larry, an esteemed hunter who now mostly shot moving pictures, and I was impressed both with what he'd said and what he hadn't said. Perhaps he was one of the ones who could have at least something in life both ways—the hunted deer, shot on film, and the live deer still in the forest, unharmed.

It was eerie, holding the Winchester in my hands; its proportions were so much like the rifle of my childhood, I could almost have been that child I thought I could not recover, could not even consider recovering, through so crude a maneuver as buying a gun. I thought then of my own history of violence. Like that of most suburban kids, it was brief, and centered around childhood; I was too well-behaved, and too fearful, as a teenager to risk much. But when I was three, I punched out my brother's best friend's front teeth as he taunted me on the cellar stairs—an excellent, direct hit. I have a vague memory of the event; my mother says that his tears and blood didn't faze me at all. When I was four or five, and my best friend Donald was tormenting me by hitting me repeatedly with a tree limb, I darted under the sharp branches and grabbed his ankle, sinking my teeth into his flesh as far as they would go. Dropping the branch, he screamed in pain and horror, half-limping, half-running home. A couple of hours later, his mother called my mother; my mother called me in to tell me what had happened. My side of the story made no difference. What had happened was that I had bitten Donald, Donald had had to go to the hospital, and his mother was wondering what kind of savage I was raising. There was talk of whether I would have to talk to the police. "What kind of savage"—I felt ashamed. And yet I felt no regret, and knew that I had been wronged. And the shame and the sense that self-defense led to shame worked their way into my marrow, where even now they remain.

Because the West Liberty Gun Club was renovating its outdoor range, I could not actually fire my Winchester until early January. It was a cold morning when I finally went down there, about 11 o'clock, and there was, finally, a break in the snowfall. I was alone. Opening the combination padlock on the roadside gate, I drove down the snowy, rutted dirt driveway, parking near the old firing area; a new concrete slab, about 50 yards away, marked the location of the soon-to-be-renovated range. Pulling a target from the target shed, I tromped down to the berm, a hundred yards from the new slab, and dug away the snow until I found the holes for the legs of the target in the frozen ground. For high-powered rifles like the Winchester, the gun club required targets to sit right against the berm, minimizing the chance that a badly-aimed bullet would go high or wide of the protective dirt wall (a few months later, in response to a new requirement from the city of West Liberty, the gun club forbade all high-powered rifle shooting, and I had to go much farther afield to practice). This meant that all my shooting would be at 100-yard targets—no more, no less. Under these conditions, it would be difficult to simulate a bear attack, but 100 yards was better than nothing.

I took aim in the 20-degree air, my breath hovering and dissipating over the black receiver of the rifle. Bracing myself, I fired. The recoil was crisp and hard, though not as hard as the shotgun I was used to; the lever action smoothly ejected the spent cartridge and inserted a new one. I emptied the magazine—six shots in all—and then walked down to the berm to inspect my work.

I had shot well, considering I was using a scopeless rifle at 100 yards. Most of the shots were a bit high and wide of center, but they had all hit the target, and their dispersion was barely a foot from one side to the other. At 75 feet, four of the six shots would have saved my life; and over time, I would aim better.

Standing in front of the target by the frozen berm, I remembered that, though heavily cowed for many years, I was a fierce fighter, had seen myself as a fierce fighter in childhood, and would fight fiercely if attacked. It would do no good to say, in the abstract, that I accepted death; I wanted to live. And if living meant shooting an attacking animal—or, lacking a rifle, standing my ground and, if necessary, attacking it with anything (an ice axe, a knife, stones) despite the obvious futility—I would do that.

In this way, the rifle impelled me toward the kind of elemental choice that seemed generally, to me, laden with despair. To shoot to kill was not to be on receptive terms with nature. Yet it was to be fiercely alive, to affirm the rightness of one's own presence, and as I considered this I began to wonder whether this was the fundamental appeal of human violence. Was violence an ultimate response to the infuriating tragedy of choice? Overwhelmed by the desire to one kind of person and another, to be good and to be powerful, to be true to oneself and true to others, to be living and to be dead, one chooses in extreme situations the horror of an absolute: I am on this side of the line, the perpetrator says, and the victim is on the other. I myself refuse to be a victim to irreconcilable desires; in violence I say, "I am." It is the opposite of the deific act of creation, but ironically, because it is an opposite, it has a unifying power that ordinary human life cannot provide. No wonder so many violent men and women, interrogated about their crimes, describe a first, initial sense of release or peace. This is senseless to ordinary minds, a sign of serious deviance. But in more elemental terms, it makes a great deal of sense.

Fighting fiercely for my life against a bear, I would be, as Andy Russell says, wilder than the bear, more full of death—but more full of life than I had ever been. Yet, seeing these words, I wonder if it is really possible to quantify this instinct to live or die, to attach the word "more" to it. What I know now, thinking toward that end, is that I am unresolved; that I am not easily a part of the human world or the natural world; that I do expect to live with something and its opposite or complement, and will attempt this over and over, despite failures; that I do distrust death; that I do distrust the sanitized language of religion and of the spirit.

Curiously, the men I most admired as a child were unresolved in the same way: Chuck Connors; Merlin the magician; and, in my most private moments, Elijah, the miracle of my Sunday School education, the man who did not see death, but was lifted into heaven through a whirlwind on a chariot of fire. It is strange to think this now, so rooted in the earth as I am and so far from a spiritual home. But perhaps my take on these men serves this January day, with Alaska far away yet near in thought, and the spirit animal of the bear still riddled with paradoxes.

I can see the Winchester gleaming in the winter light as I walk back to the shooters' bench. It is something beautiful and deadly, something apart from me and something I love. And I think: if I could be at once as single-minded and as unresolved as Elijah was, even death would be no enemy. Admittedly, I am far from that; and if my faith in Elijah's miracle is a romantic fantasy, then a fatal mauling could be one antidote to my foolishness. But if my faith corresponds to something fundamentally real, then I can trust the wilderness and the bear who haunts me, whether—how can I bring myself to say this?—whether I live or die, whether or not I am a rifleman.

Thomas Simmons

The Woman Who Married a Bear

Along the Pacific northwest coast, from Vancouver Island north to what is now southeastern Alaska, two major bear myths have dominated the spiritual life of the Tlingit, Tsimshian and Haida tribes. In one of these, a man who marries a bear and has children by her returns to his human wife. The bear mother warns him to provide food only for his bear children, but he breaks this rule and the bears kill him. In the other myth, which John Bierhorst describes (in *The Mythology of North America*) as "a much greater favorite," the story goes this way: "The heroine, a haughty young woman, is abducted by a grizzly or brown bear and becomes the mother of his children. With his knowledge, she betrays him, sending a signal to her brothers, who become his killers." This second version, known as the Bear Mother myth, has important variants—not only within the native cultures but within the anglo culture as well, for Gary Snyder includes a version of it in his 1990 *The Practice of the Wild*, and R. Edward Grumbine adapts that version for his 1992 *Ghost Bears*, as follows:

"Once upon a time there was a girl out picking berries. She was a young girl, strong, and used to having her own way. One afternoon, she stayed late picking berries and everyone else went home. She spilled her basket and was gathering them up. A tall, handsome man appeared. He helped her and said, 'Let's keep picking till dark. I know good places and will take you home.' They picked together in the gathering dusk. Then it was dark. They built a fire, roasted meat, and ate. They slept by the fire. The next day they began picking berries again but the girl thought about home. 'I want to go home, now,' she said. The man slapped her on the head and circled her head with his finger the way the sun circles the Earth. Then she lost track of time and they traveled and picked berries for a long while.

"He was just like a human, but she thought he might be a bear. They traveled a long while. It was fall now. It was turning cold. She knew that he was a grizzly bear. 'It's time to dig a winter lodge,' he said. 'Get some brush for our bed.' He began to dig into the side of the mountain. She collected fir boughs but she left a sign for her brothers, too. 'That brush is no good,' he said, 'and you have left a mark to guide your brothers here. We must go.' They traveled up the valley to a new place. He began to dig again and she collected brush. This time, she brought the proper bedding. But she also left a sign. She knew that her brothers would hunt the valley in the spring and find their den.

"During the winter, she bore two babies, a girl and a boy, just when bears have their cubs. The winter was very long. One time she woke to hear her husband singing. He was a shaman. 'Before the snow is gone your brothers will come for me—I will fight them!' he said. 'No! No!' she replied. 'They are your relations now, you cannot kill them.' 'All right, I will let them come,' he said. But later, he was singing again. 'If they come, if they kill me because I cannot fight them, get from them my skull and tail. Burn my head and tail in a fire and sing my song till nothing but ashes remains.' Then they slept. Spring was coming.

"Now he was singing again. Now the dogs were barking and the brothers were in the valley hunting. 'They are coming! I will fight them to the death!' 'No, you must not! Who will take care of the children if they lose both their uncles? You must let them come.' 'I am taking down my knives,' he replied. He was a very large grizzly bear. 'I am going now.' He left the den and was silent for a long time.

"The woman left the den. She came out into the spring light. Her brothers had killed the grizzly bear. They found her on the mountainside. 'You have killed your brother-in-law,' she said. 'Save the head and tail for me.'

"She went home to her family after being gone a year. They hardly recognized her. That night, she built a great fire and burned the grizzly's skull and tail and sang his song. She could not stay in her mother's house. She built a separate camp nearby for herself and her children. In the fall as the air turned cold, she finally came into her mother's lodge. It was not easy for her to do this.

"Next spring, her brothers killed a female grizzly bear with two cubs. They wanted their sister and her children to wear the hides and pretend they were bears. 'No, I cannot do that or I'll turn into a bear forever,' she said. But her brothers would not listen. They pestered her. They wanted her to put on the hide. Then they snuck up from behind and threw the hides over them. She turned into a big grizzly bear and walked on all fours. Then she had to fight them. She killed her family, sparing only her youngest brother. Tears were streaming down her face. Then she took her children, her cubs, and went back into the mountains, far away."

Even a quick reading exposes central differences between this version and Bierhorst's. The girl is not "haughty," as she is in the Bierhorst version. Although she is "strong, and used to having her own way," no negative connotation necessarily arises from this. On the contrary, she is described as a young woman who trusts her own mind. And while the young woman is, by our standards, abducted, it is an abduction preceded by choice. She chooses to pick berries until dark, she chooses to share her dinner with the "tall, handsome man," and she sleeps with him by the fire. His deception is important, but it is equally important to understand that it is a deception of species rather than of temperament: as a man or as a bear, he is of the same character, and thus at a fundamental level does not deceive her about who he is. When, the next day, he slaps her on the head, the violence of the act co-exists with its ritual quality—the slap preceding his circling of her head "the way the sun circles the earth." In Snyder's version, the willingness of the woman to stay, despite her uncertainty about whether her mate was a man or a bear, is important: "she stayed with him," Snyder says, "as long as he was good to her."

Finally, and most important, the myth does not end with the woman's brothers killing the bear. It ends with the woman killing her family, "sparing only her youngest brother." The focus in this version of the myth is clearly on the bear's sense of the inevitability of his fate, the woman's deep investment in the life of the bear, and her relatives' fatal insistence that she choose to be either a woman or a bear—but not both.

Interestingly, the actual source for Grumbine's abridged version is not Snyder, but rather Maria Johns, a member of the Tlingit tribe who was born sometime in the 1880's. Snyder takes his text from Johns' telling of the myth to Catherine McClellan; this version, along with eleven others, was originally published in McClellan's 1970 *The Woman Who Married a Bear: A Masterpiece of Indian Oral Tradition*. The myth that Grumbine credits tribally *via* Snyder, then, is actually one version from a specific native American woman who herself began to mediate between native American and anglo culture around the turn of the century.

For Grumbine the myth offers archaic evidence for the close relationship between humans and bears. For Snyder the myth performs a somewhat different, perhaps larger, service, raising the question of how we live in two worlds that, as he suggests (or is it Johns who suggests this?) are really one. The reality, however, is that one person, who is neither Snyder nor Grumbine, lies behind this myth. Behind her lies her tribe; ahead of her lie men and women who will take the myth for their own purposes. The temptation, then, is to universalize the myth, to see it as almost infinitely impersonal and transportable. But there is, as it turns out, a danger in overlooking the personal. In the end it is Maria Johns, and not those who follow her, whose guidance becomes indispensable.

II

We know that, except in those accidental moments when love coincides with social convention, love is a rule-breaker. Maria Johns, talking of the Bear Mother myth, describes it this way:

> Most people know that breaking rules is bad, and when they do it in a sneaky way they feel they're doing wrong. Some people break rules because of muddy hearts and greed. Some people are clear, and break the rules because they want to *know*. They also understand that there's a price to pay, and won't complain.

For Johns, knowledge is akin to love: to love is to desire above all to *know*, and this is the source of our troubles. It was, however, the source of—let us say

Job's—redemption as well as his trouble; for he loved God so greatly that he wanted to know what God knew. God's questions confirmed the legitimacy of Job's love. The selves that supercede whatever we consider, at any given point, to be *our* self emerge from our own, passionate need to know. This need may be internal, but it is also the creation calling us, saying, "You are more than that, you are more than that: *find out*." Thus in any person's life there are implicitly multiple lives, multiple worlds, and it may be impossible to cross among them without disrupting the lives of those whose need to cross such borders is not as intense, or not as intense at the same time.

Like Grumbine and Snyder, Maria Johns knows that "The Woman Who Married a Bear" is about the mythic interweaving of the bear world and the human—about the symbiosis between creatures, and about the need to cherish forms of life whose mysteries inhabit our dreams and imaginings. But Johns' story is also about love, about the undeniable impulsion to transform oneself; and it is about lost faith, since—to be honest about this—the idea of a woman becoming a bear, or a bear becoming a shaman-man, seems impossible to those of us raised in a world of reason and empirical science. It is Johns' clear-eyed grieving for this loss of faith that shapes her story differently, that gives it different implications from what one finds in Snyder's version (for it is important to understand that Snyder silently amends portions of the myth and Johns' commentary, so that one must read very carefully, with some background knowledge, to tell where Snyder has chosen for Johns to leave off and for Snyder to begin) or in Grumbine's. And this, most of all, matters to me because the bear that has been haunting my life has not been merely a creature of the wild, but a creature of love and aloneness—a creature of the wilderness that exists when something essential in one's being has been destroyed, and something else must be created to fill its place.

When I hear the voice of Maria Johns, who died more than 50 years ago, behind the story of the woman who married a bear, I know that all the selves and borders we cherish must ultimately be broken down, and broken down, and broken down, and that the terrors and visions that ensue from this do not invalidate the devotion that we give to these borders.

In the end, we become what we grieve most ardently.

III

What I would like to say is: I have learned to live as the bear mother lived. The bear who came to me in a gust of wind in Alaska two years ago made clear what had caused me such confusion and doubt, and I saw that I could not go back to my own life. As much pain as that separation caused me and my wife and children, it was a necessary separation, because I had seen a reality that drew me further than I had ever traveled, and my new self could not be put to death in service to the old.

But I cannot say this. For the reality is far more complex than the myth. The reality is that I married for love, or rather for a love and strife almost as familiar to me as breathing. I married a woman I had fallen in love with in high school; I had broken up with her, and she with me, enough times for each of us to seem to know the other's darker shadows. "Love" came to seem a less relevant word than "knowledge." Of course we loved each other; it was a given. In our wedding ceremony, which my sister the Episcopalian priest let us write, we did not pledge ourselves to each other "until death do us part." We pledged ourselves "for as long as this love is our guide," an anapestic phrase that signaled our trust in the straightforwardness of love. As long as it lasted, we would last; if it ended, we would go as our separate souls directed. This was a beautiful child's hopefulness, but it indicated not so much naivete as our mutual trust. We knew each other; on that basis we would make our way confidently through the world.

But selves that know each other in a relatively secure context, with supportive family and decent incomes and a sense of rootedness in the world, are not the same as lost and isolated selves, terrified of the prospect of unemployment and the loss of all that they have worked for, frightened that they and their children may be homeless, that they may be failures, that their dreams may prove illusory and meaningless. It seems to me that more dreams lurked in my own heart than I had ever given voice to in the early years of my marriage, and these bore relatively little relation to the life I had come to live. The same may have been true for Lesley, though she concealed them perhaps even more successfully than I. Why did we do this? Because we had seen our clear paths in the particular culture where we occupied particular stations, those of the young intelligensia, and we had no reason to abdicate. It was clear from some of our friends' lives that abdication brought confusion, aimlessness, and harm. And while confusion, aimlessness, and harm are all part of the history of spiritual experience in the world, we shied from these as though from a conversion to another faith.

It might seem utterly predictable, then, that in the nadir of our recent lives— the summer and fall of 1991, when we were slipping meteorically into debt, when I had gone from nearly being dismissed to being promoted at MIT (but with only a "fair to good" chance of tenure, code words explained to me, perhaps erroneously, as meaning "find another job"), when Lesley had almost lost hope of finishing her dissertation, when we were both struggling to care for two small children, when an ABC correspondent revealed to me that the Christian Science church had compiled a dossier on me in order to leak any potentially damaging rumors about my life to the press (and had, in fact, "leaked" my marital problems and depression to this correspondent)—in this nadir, some passionate break would have to occur. We were mired, trapped in ways that knowledge could not help. We needed a fierce escape, as various friends and acquaintances observed in retrospect. Either of us was, they said, ripe for an explosion of romance.

Yet what actually occurred was no stereotypical explosion of romance. The person who arrived with her consoling presence spoke to me in a language I had first heard far back in my childhood and had almost forgotten—a language of private hope whose syllables all registered an assurance that the world, however evil it might be, had at its source certain beautiful refuges that we could imagine, name, and reach. And while I might have wanted this to be a sexual revelation, it was not. It was a revelation of the kind one experiences when, having been chronically ill, one looks to the new day and sees, finally, the dawn of one's own healed self.

If I was the bear, this soulmate was the young woman picking berries and jumping over the scat, despite everyone's warning. And yet we could easily have played the opposite roles: she was, at times, shamanic, while I was all too human. But the nature of a formal arrangement of human love—a compact between one self and another to "love, honor, and cherish"—makes it virtually impossible for such an ambiguous, alternative relationship to exist without great pain for everyone involved. The one character missing from the Bear Mother myth, after all, is a human husband for the young woman or a bear-lover for the grizzly—one who has loved and trusted and known her mate, only to see that closeness evaporate as the mate finds some more familiar self through the benedictions of another. For that third character, that spouse, life becomes a story of betrayal and jealousy, as Diane Middlebrook writes:

> Jealousy fans the night, a moth whose rapid wings
> Sift their dust into the light that falls
> Along your arm extended careless
> And averted face;
> The wings are mine; in rage like flame I plan
> The resolute infliction of my pain.

I had made a formal enemy of the woman I had married, and with whom I had worked for so many years to make a life, though its wounds had now become palpable. Eleven years earlier, we had agreed before God that we would honor love by remaining together only so long as that love was our guide. Yet the apparent collapse of that love did not make our parting any easier. We had been fools to the nature of love.

Did I pray? Yes. I prayed at night for release from these torments of love, and though I knew that, if I truly believed in God, my wisdom compared to His was less than miniscule, still I prayed for a specific end—that I might be released from my failed marriage to move toward a way of thinking and loving that this new soulmate had offered me. It might have been helpful at that point to remember Joel Goldsmith's admonishments about praying *for* anything, but one's desperation tends to invent dialogues when the need to be silent is imperative. God was thus silent in word and deed, as far as I could tell in my secretly unreceptive state, and the tragedies of desire and sadness and jealousy twisted out of my control, until eventually I was simply alone.

In the Bear Mother myth, this kind of aloneness comes only after a great tragedy—after the brothers have forced the identity of the bear upon their sister, and she turns and kills all but one of them. But what was it the brothers insisted? They insisted that she choose—that she be part of their family, or part of the bear's family. In this kind of choice one hears the echo of marriage: cleave to me, and not to the other; or to the other, and not to me. Our culture (and the Tlingit's as well) presumes that this is good, for our deepest allegiances cannot, apparently, run beyond the course of a single family. Yet the Tlingit also saw that this insistence on either/or can lead to disaster; some matters of the heart are also matters of spirit, and cannot be constrained without deep danger.

When the brothers throw the bearskin over their sister, after having killed the bear who slept with her, they marry her to the world of the bears, and she kills them because she knows she should not have been so wed. It was in her nature to move between the two, as it was the nature of the bear-shaman whom the brothers killed. Her ensuing isolation is her tragedy and her blessing, and the way the myth falls silent following her departure tells us that we cannot gain access to her world as long was we approve of the brothers' deeds—that is, as long as we approve of the either/or culture in which we, and most humans, live. And yet we are fully conditioned from childhood on to believe that the brothers' course of action is the right one.

What kind of world (I ask this now, as I have for three years) makes love the vehicle for such tragedy? How can it be that the most powerful force of transformation and hope can leave us in terror? What else is there to trust in, if not in love? And when we are in love, as Anne Sexton says, "right down to the toes," and love still creates nightmarish chaos and isolation, what is it that we have learned about the world? That God must destroy us in order to save us? That our God is really the God of My Lai?

This I remember from childhood: there were times when I prayed, or my mother prayed, or Christian Science practitioners prayed, and an extraordinary peace descended upon me when I was sick or miserable—a knowing more powerful than anything I usually knew, a knowing as powerful as feeling. I knew that I was cherished, and that I lived in harmony with the universe. These were big words for a relatively small child, but they were my words (or, rather, Mary Baker Eddy's words on my lips), and they expressed my astonished sense of comfort. And then, slowly, I would recover from whatever sadness or discontent possessed me. Although I do not recall ever having been healed in childhood of a physical illness through prayer, I do recall feeling something that did not seem to me to have a human origin—or if it did, it was an origin usually obscured from my sight. Somewhere, across the continuum of species, across the lives of ants and bees and locusts and cats and dogs and pigs and chimpanzees and humans, a power descended that felt like "a new knowledge of reality." And that power brought peace to all it touched. It was at once transforming and affirming; it did not make me choose between my "human" life and a "spiritual" life. There was only life.

Was that, then, the sum of love? If so, why did it come so rarely? And why, now, does it seem so clearly to have an explosive corollary, a version that leads us to whomever we most need and want and then denies us fulfillment? Is it foolish to ask why we are ruined, spiritually, over and over again, though our efforts and our faith be sincere?

I have, again, no words to answer these questions directly. I must again go out and around the subject, because I am on the point of such rage that all words fail. A rage against God is a bad thing, unless one has the heart of Job. And can one ever say that—"I have the heart of Job"? Surely the statement itself confirms the lie, for one has such a heart not by averring it but by asking insistent and passionate questions, and sticking around for a reply. Nevertheless, as my questions bear some relation to Job's, I would like to look at one particular implication of this power of love that I once felt, crossing "the continuum of species."

IV

Everything has a language. Though Job's outrage reflects the experience of a man who has lived blamelessly, and who thus deserved neither the destruction of his family or the pious pontificating of his companions, it also implies something more fundamental: the whole of creation hears him. It is the whole order of creation, including its creator, and not simply a moral matter between God and man, that Job calls into question. This is what finally silences Bildad, Zophar, and Eliphaz, and causes God utterly to ignore the god-mimicking fury of Elihu. When God speaks out of the whirlwind, He speaks, not in defense of Himself, but in defense of the whole creation. And while it would appear that His series of questions humbles Job, it is also His way of affirming for Job that He *does* hear: the unanswered question is evidence, not of cosmic coldness, but of God's presence.

To this terrible paradox, seemingly comfortless to us, Job answers, "I know that thou canst do every thing, and that no thought can be witholden from thee." Job is comforted, not as a creature cowed by his ignorance, but as one who has learned to equate the mysteries of the creation with the divine presence. God is personal in the language of creation; only in the formulaic language of well-meaning human beings is He abstract, distant. But to find this divine personality,

Job must transgress by rebelling against human advice. Moreover, he must understand language in a fundamentally different way from other humans. For Job, God's questions *are* answers; they imply a continuity between two seemingly unbridgeable worlds.

If I ask again, then, the two questions with which I began this journey—"Who are you, and what do you love?"—I find that I am further from comfort than I had imagined. For it is not these questions, finally, that matter: the furious questions, the questions of utter outrage, are the ones that matter, that set some context for a response: "What kind of world is this, in which love causes such damage?" "If God is love, is God Himself pure blasphemy?"

Asking this again and again, like a mantra or a prayer, from day to day, I find myself on one particular day in the Botany-Chemistry Library at the University of Iowa, where, among the low ceilings and metal shelves full of books, I take down an edition of Helena Curtis' *Biology* and begin to read. I read portions of this book many years ago with little interest, since I believed that the world was spiritual and that physical biology was a self-defeating mythology, a clever lie. Thus it is a strange thing, now, to stare at the double-stranded helix of deoxyribonucleic acid, DNA, with its railings of sugar-phosphate units, its rungs of purines and pyramidines—and to know, as little as I know of biology, that this model of life speaks on earth almost as authoritatively as a myth of God. What does it mean that I think this? It means, according to A. Young in his 1980 "Dimensions of Medical Rationality," that I have developed an "internalizing belief system," characteristic of western societies, in which I now look at the molecular level for meaning and for healing. I am wedded to the gene as the inner sanctum of life. And yet I know this not to be true, despite all that I have done to make it true; for I was raised, as many native Americans are raised, in a religion with an "externalizing belief system," in which causes and effects are macrocosmic and extend into the realm of myth (in my case, this was the myth of the powerfully illusory material world, which spirit ultimately would vanquish).

For me, adult knowledge and the disappointments of my childhood religion came together electrically in the metaphor, if not the physical reality, of the double helix. One strand of the double helix always implicates God, and—as strange as it may sound—implicates a border-crossing to the material of the genome, where spirit and matter reside at the genetic center of life, and where the chemical rungs themselves are the woman who married a bear, crossing over into another world so that both realities may have their due.

Even out of this genetic material, then, I am inclined to create a myth. But what does this have to do with love? To see the creation potentially divided against itself even at the level of the gene is to see a few patterns and a few mutations repeated over and over, varied more and more, moving out toward chaos even as the basic substance remains unchanged. Love and lovers remain, and their treasure makes life possible, and their troubles multiply beyond number, on into death, into the world of spirit; but that world is not separate from this world, for it too is forecast in the essential material of life, and all of our imaginings have their root authority in something as tiny and internal as a gene or as vast and external as a deity. Or rather: the two interpenetrate each other, as woman and bear, or bear woman. It is a vision accessible only to questions—and not only reverential questions, but scoffing questions, questions based in disbelief and ridicule, questions based in revulsion.

Where, then, is the comfort we must have from love, the comfort we apparently need to survive? And how (you may well ask) did I come to this view of life, having intended to write primarily about love? Isn't what I have written here simply a deflection of feelings too painful finally to confront? What about the love I lost—and the vision of life with it? And what of the love I now have?

V

For days now I have wanted to stop my reading, my comparisons of myths and sources, and simply say: "I want to write about love! I want to write about love!" But I have found over and over that, sitting down with love as my theme, I have failed to find the words. They have hidden from me. And thus I have come at the subject by way of a myth about bears—and not only that; by way of a myth that means somewhat different things to different people, so that even it, as a medium for my story, has an ambiguous quality. Two thousand and three thousand years ago, in ancient Roman and Greek culture, poets invoked specific muses to aid them in their work. My work, now, appears unlikely to come to any fruition unless I invoke a muse of ambiguity, with her heart significantly veiled and given to two very different cultures. My readers who detest ambiguity will thus be driven from this essay. Those who suspect my direction from what has already been said, however, will also have some intuition about why they want to read on.

I first came to the Bear Mother myth *via* Edward Grumbine's book. And while it might appear, from what I have written in this book so far, that I took up Grumbine's work because of my primary concern about damaged ecosystems and the larger damage between humans and the natural world, this is not actually true. I bought *Ghost Bears* because, in Prairie Lights Bookstore in Iowa City in May 1994, I happened to be drawn to the book's fog-bound cover photograph of the Cascades, which reminded me so much of Crow Pass in Alaska, and when I picked up the book I happened to turn to page 69, where Grumbine begins "The Bear Mother Myth." When I read this myth, I knew that it was about nothing more than love, and that it answered a question—or at least redefined the question—in a way I had been yearning for for years. I gave little thought, at that time, regrettably, to the Tlingit culture that spawned this myth, except by way of gratitude for what I thought to be a gratifyingly non-Western source. I was not even especially interested in the link between people and bears, although it did strike me as strange that the ghostly presence of a bear at Crow Pass two years before had become such a string back through the labyrinth of my life. I was not, after all, a naturalist. And yet, reading "The Bear Mother Myth," I saw myself in Grumbine's book.

Or, rather, I should say: I saw myself in the bear and the young woman. For both of them were not single selves, but double or multiple selves. The bear was not only a bear, but a man (Johns makes it even clearer that he looked like a bear only when he was digging; "the rest of the time he looked like a human being"). He was also a shaman, a man of spirit whose bear identity was integral to his power. And the young woman who became his companion, though she remained a young woman (her brothers recognized her and brought her home), also developed a profound spiritual loyalty to her mate. She could not go back into her mother's house. Whatever passed between these two creatures made them so different that they defied creaturely categories. The were—to use an expression from my childhood—transformed by love.

But this made them dangerous to those who were not similarly transformed. The woman's brothers particularly could not abide the thought that their sister was both one kind of creature and another—one self and another. In fact, given the woman's transformation, it is clear that the word "self" comes under implicit attack in this myth: there is always only a provisional self, and it is the nature of love on earth to elide this self into other versions of self to show how our reality is never fixed or static, but always becoming. The bear extended the woman's reality—her sensuality, her understanding of the creation, her sense of time, her sense of spiritual power. And she confirmed his expansive presence in the human world. Neither of these two could be described in terms of a single self, for such a self could at best be a starting point.

Yet it appears that some people are conscious of having only one self, of being only one kind of creature. The woman's brothers are such people. They are not bad people; on the contrary, they are devoted to their family, protective, loving—they can scarcely be criticized. Their only failing is their lack of that kind of imagination which makes it possible to hold two apparently contradictory realities in mind at the same time. That is an exceptionally advanced form of imagination, acquired not through intellect but through something innate or instinctual, and it is rare. When it manifests itself—as it did in the sister and the bear—it threatens anyone who adheres to a single identity. To protect their own sense of reality, the brothers must insist that the others conform to a model of the single self—must be either this or that, either woman or bear.

And so the brothers cajole and pester and pursue their sister, urging her to put on the skin of another bear they have killed, urging her to be that one self—a self finally different from their own, so that they do not have to tolerate the idea of multiple selves within a single family. The sister refuses, cherishing her ambiguity. Moreover, she knows that to be defined one way or another will be fatal to her relationship with her human family; it will illuminate the gulf between them. When the brothers throw the bearskin over her, her worst fears come true (for she wishes them no ill): she destroys them, because they have forced an absolute separation from her—a separation not only from themselves, but from her own multi-selved being. They have come closer to destroying her than they know, but because it is their own crippled imagination that they draw on for power, they invite their own deaths. She goes on to live as a bear in the wilderness of human rejection. And who she becomes and what she knows is closed to us from then on.

If we are truly attentive to the implications of love, we can say that we are "one self" only for a certain period of time under certain circumstances. There are always other versions of ourselves yearning to be born, yearning to become conscious in order to bring us more centrally into the heart of creation. Thus, paradoxically, whenever we love, we are saying two things to the beloved: I love you; and I will leave you. Whoever it is you have helped me to be will need to be another self along the way; the same will be true of you. The leaving may or may not be traumatic; we may leave our respective selves along parallel lines, our new selves a further complement to our original love; but this is not a given. We love in a long or short passage toward a greater love that we cannot name, that may not be personal, that may be finally what we now call a wilderness.

When that leaving of old selves does turn out to be mutual or parallel, it means what we most crave in romantic love: some people do not leave each other, nor do they remain locked into a single sense of self. They move outward into the world, assuming and shedding careers and fantasies and faiths, tracking each other as they move into dark privacies of doubt, and yet bringing each other along, so that at some intermediate point these two explorers emerge as different people with deeply intertwined pasts, cherishing each other as far as knowledge and love permit. How does this happen? Why does it not happen all the time?

I do not know. And yet it does strike me that something from my childhood religion, which I feared and raged against for so long, now seems more true than I once imagined. We live in an accidental world. Though not governed by random force, as I was instructed in the most clumsy and foolish of my religious teachings, it is enmeshed in chaos; the results of this chaos sometimes are lovely, sometimes are dreadful beyond description. In the Newtonian version of this world, the fall of a thousand apples demonstrates gravity; but if those apples fall because of a disease, preventing the farmer from harvesting any crop and ruining him financially, this proves nothing but the accidental interplay of physical, biological, and economic forces. Or, from another perspective: we may think of the weather in a certain geographic region as having, as Robert Frost says, "roughly zones" of temperature, rainfall, and snowfall, which we can rely on as "natural law" or "acts of God"—even though, as James Gleick observes in

Chaos, what we call patterns diverge so widely over time that they cannot finally be called patterns at all.

In love, as well, accident rules. A million marriages in a particular year signal the power of human desire to come together in love; if 50% of those end in divorce, is love to blame? Or is it rather the nature of desire to outstrip compatibility, so that all adventures in love are experiments, with half of them doomed to failure? We must know in our secret, skeptical hearts that the latter version is true. In fact, what we all love fails far more than half the time; for behind the million relationships that come to the altar or the justice of the peace lie millions more that died somewhere along the way. And if certain versions of aloneness make us particularly sad—the old man or woman, for example, subsisting in a single room with a hotplate and tiny refrigerator, with no family or lover, with no pet, with no one—it may be because we so easily see ourselves in that role, because we know so well the powerful accident of love. There is nothing in this world to suggest that two people who fall in love will necessarily help each other move through the confusions of the self to some equilibrium. That it happens may be a miracle; but, again in natural terms, it is aberrant.

Yet love *is* real: it leaves an ineradicable impression upon us, like the impression of a particularly powerful eucharist or vision of holiness. We see it; we recognize it; but we cannot create it as we create a poem, say, or a 747. Thus we virtually invite ourselves to occupy the role of the charitable brothers of the bear mother, who must have things one way or the other in order to confirm the limits of human experience. But that is the worst faithlessness. It leads to our own deaths. It is, on the whole, incredible how well and how readily we assent to these deaths.

Primates

In August 1979, just before I wrapped up my job as a summer intern at the *Christian Science Monitor*, Henrietta Buckmaster invited me to her house for dinner. As editor of "The Home Forum," the *Monitor*'s daily double-page spread of art and literature, Henrietta had been the first person to publish my poetry and essays when I was a college senior in 1977. She had also set a tone of egalitarian compassion for the page that had always impressed me. "The Home Forum" published some of the worst poetry and essays I had ever read, but it also published some of the best (interestingly, it was Sylvia Plath's first major venue in the early 1950's, and poets as celebrated as William Stafford or as distinctively obscure as Rosemary Cobham could often be found there). For several years it had intrigued me to try to second-guess the editor's decisions.

Now I knew her personally, having worked closely with her over the summer even as I performed the other tasks of an intern—distributing wire copy (in the days when we still had "wire copy" coming in over a teletype, still a decade before the Internet), riding shotgun on the copy desk, taking incoming stories over the phone—and I had come to understand why so many people on the paper spoke of her with a combination of awe, exasperation, and deep affection. Henrietta could be forbiddingly masterful, but she could forgive and bless with the egoless confidence of a child. I had seen her bring peace to tearful colleagues—the *Monitor* was not always a harmonious place—in a way that I usually attributed to successful Christian Science practitioners. I had also seen her confront more senior editors over some matter that brought out her staunch and righteous defiance. It had been a great privilege to come to know her.

Henrietta had been crippled early by polio, which Christian Science had never healed, although she in no way saw this as criticism of the religion. She walked laboriously and somewhat loudly with the aid of two metal canes. In the dim hallway of her ground-floor condominium on Clearway Street in Boston, just behind what was then the Christian Science Publishing Society with its huge presses humming in the basement, I had to be careful not to knock her over by moving too swiftly behind her.

As she brought me into her small, bright kitchen, it seemed for a moment as if she had some kind of fancy wallpaper that moved or shimmered in the light. But of course that was only a form of shock that made me briefly overlook what I was actually seeing: cockroaches. Of all the American cities I have lived in, Boston is the most overwhelmed with roaches, and the Back Bay area near the Christian Science Center is particularly bad. In my own apartment, a few blocks away, my roommates and I had a nightly ritual after coming back from dinner or a movie. Removing our shoes before opening the door, we would walk very quietly in our socks into the kitchen, where we would place ourselves at three different points—by the sink, the stove countertop, the counter below the cupboards. One of us would have his finger on the light switch. We'd all count—"one, two, THREE"—and as light flooded the room we'd slam our shoes down on every flat surface in the kitchen. In that period of two or three seconds, hundreds of roaches would try to scuttle to safety; once, sweeping up afterwards, we counted sixty roach carcasses. That was life on Commonwealth Avenue in Boston in 1979.

Roaches were all over Henrietta's condominum—on the floors, the counters, even the walls—which made me a little uncomfortable, despite my considerable experience with them. Distracted for a minute as I swept a couple of them off a chair, I said, "These things are horrible. My roommates and I have been doing everything—spraying, roach hotels—we still can't stop them."

"I don't try to stop them," Henrietta said.

That's when I noticed that several roaches were crawling on her.

She was wearing a Tahitian floral print housedress, and the dark brownish-silvery sheen of the insects as they climbed up her wide back made me increasingly uncomfortable. I sat quite still.

"I don't think one should kill animals without need," she said, as she limped to the other side of the kitchen, leaned her canes against the counter, and pulled a casserole from the oven with thick hotpads.

"There are a couple of...do you want me to, ah...I have a little trouble with roaches crawling on people," I said.

"Do you," she said. "Well, these won't cause any harm."

The casserole, interestingly enough, was fish stew. Because I have some kind of allergy to fish—whether physical or emotional I've never determined, though years of having my mother shove cod liver oil down my throat in a vain and unspiritual attempt to ward off colds may have had something to do with it—I was unable to do much more than slide the bits of fish around and behind clumps of peeled potatoes and zucchini. The small dining room where we ate felt rather close, yet a nice breeze came through the house, and if I looked only at Henrietta's face I found that I could almost forget the presence of the roaches on her breasts and shoulders. She had a stunning face—filled with care, even with torment, but not worn by it; illuminated, in fact, so that her eyes, which would have been piercing in any case, appeared at once fierce and depthless. We talked about everything, it seemed—the poems of William Stafford; the relation between physical healing and spiritual insight; the prospects for Africa in the 21st century; the future of the *Monitor* ; my future as a college English instructor at Stanford in the fall. As we discussed some particularly cruel things that the chairman of the Board of Directors of the Christian Science Church had said to me earlier in the summer during a dispute about a particular church policy,

Henrietta exuded calm. She talked about the kind of risktaking that requires forgiveness and precedes blessedness. And we talked about animals.

"I have the silliest arguments with my co-workers about animals," she said. "Some of them don't think that animals have souls at all. Roy Barnacle, you know, in the wire room, doesn't even think they're real, spiritually speaking. They're just food to him, or targets."

"But they do have souls," she said. "They are God's creatures, just as we are."

Although, of all the things that Henrietta said to me that night—the last night I was ever to see her—this comment about animals did not rank particularly high, it nevertheless stayed with me longer than I suspected it would. I found it coming back to mind as the crux of something, a troubling point whose disturbance I could not really track. I was not on the way to becoming a zoologist or paleontologist; her other observations that night should have stuck much closer to my heart. But it keep slipping back into mind—this business of animals having souls. Though I knew that, to more practical, empirical, or sober-minded people, the phrase was virtually nonsensical, I knew what Henrietta had meant. Or at least I thought I did. But the more I thought about it, the more I began to wonder.

Was an animal soul in some way equivalent to a human soul? If an animal had a soul, could it love? Did that make the love of a gorilla for its offspring equivalent to the love of a human mother or father for its offspring? Was it the same for a dog? A cat? A pig? How far down the line could you go? Did fish have souls? Were they souls of a different kind from human souls—essences, though not endowed with the power of love? Sixteen years later, Daniel Dennett would briefly summarize these questions in his tedious yet celebrated book *Darwin's Dangerous Idea*, but no such summary existed then, and even if it had, my background almost certainly would have prevented me from reading it. These questions thus took their toll quickly, leading me into intellectual chaos, and so I cut them away, preferring the comfort of what I felt to be a kind of instinctive rightness to Henrietta's observation: what we and animals share of the creation is shared at a common source.

Because it was obviously ungettable-at, that common source interested me a great deal over the next couple of years. Fourteen months after my dinner with Henrietta, as I stood by my mother's fresh grave in Palo Alto, California, I read a poem by Wendell Berry called "To the Unseeable Animal." It began with an epigraph from Berry's daughter: "I hope there's an animal somewhere that nobody has ever seen," she says. "And I hope nobody ever sees it." I read the epigraph to the plain morning air of death, and then the poem:

Thomas Simmons

> Being, whose flesh dissolves
> at our glance, knower
> of the secret sums and measures,
> you are always here,
> dwelling in the oldest sycamores,
> visiting the faithful springs
> when they are dark and the foxes
> have crept to their edges.
> I have come upon pools
> in streams, places overgrown
> with the woods' shadow,
> where I knew you had rested,
> watching the little fish
> hang still in the flow;
> as I approached they seemed
> particles of your clear mind
> disappearing among the rocks.
> I have waked deep in the woods
> in the early morning, sure
> that while I slept
> your gaze passed over me.
> That we do not know you
> is your perfection
> and our hope. The darkness
> keeps us near you.

My mother, who as a Christian Scientist had seemed embarrassed by her own death, had asked for no funeral, but it was urgent for me—and for my father and sister and brother—to mark the moment in some way. As we stood by the grave, I read a poem about the clarifying comfort of darkness, and at that moment those words made more sense to me than any of the religious orthodoxies I had been taught.

It was interesting, then, about three years later, to have a chance to write about this poem in an essay on Wendell Berry for the *Christian Science Monitor*. Henrietta had commissioned me to write a number of pieces on contemporary poets—later nominated for a Pulitzer Prize in criticism—and Berry seemed an obvious choice. It was obvious to Henrietta as well, once she'd received my essay, although she hadn't before read much of Berry's work. "Thank you for the Berry piece," she wrote back in her usual hasty scrawl of acceptance, "especially 'To the Unseeable Animal.' It has confirmed something in my seeing."

A few weeks later, my housemate in Berkeley left me a note to call one of the assistant editors of "The Home Forum." When I did, I learned what in my heart I had half-expected. The features editor had killed the Berry piece, with the concurrence of the new editor-in-chief. "To the Unseeable Animal," they said, did not properly reflect the kind of Christian Science values that ought to inhabit "The Home Forum." They were willing to offer what they saw as a compromise: I could quote part of "To the Unseeable Animal" (but not the last four lines), eliminate any reference to what they called its "mysticism," and they would still run the essay. I refused. I also dictated a message to the assistant editor, which I hoped would shame the editors who had made such a shameful decision, though I knew it would not. I felt sorry for Henrietta, who had wanted so much to publish the essay and the poem, and had been, as she occasionally was, prevented. I did not know, then, that she was within two months of her own death, nor would I have believed it if someone had told me that I would learn of her death, not through an obituary or some other public announcement, or an invitation to her funeral, but only because the assistant editor, chagrined and sorrowful, decided to call me several days after her body was found. Once again, in Christian Science, silence reigned—almost.

Among my first thoughts—after the initial shock and grief and horror at the typical Christian Science response to death—was the odd realization that one poem linked my mother's death and Henrietta's. Both women cared deeply for animals; both were, in some ways, more finely animal than many humans I had met; and both had died under a veil of silence. As I read Berry's poem for solace over the next few months, I began to regret how much *knowing* I had brought to his "being" and "darkness." I thought of those words as paradoxes, with "darkness" implying "light" and "being" implying something seemingly absent yet immanent—perhaps God, Spirit, or any of the other synonyms for God in Christian Science. But whereas Christian Science was a religion heavily dependent upon the complexities of language—existing, in some ways, in language more than anywhere else—Berry's poem existed at the edge of language, as if what could not be seen also could not be spoken of. I felt the language of my religion clouding my understanding of the poem even as I grieved the loss of a mother and an editor, until finally I had to turn away both from the religion and the poem and go back to Henrietta's scrawled note, trusting that what Berry's poem had confirmed for her would, somehow, over the years, be confirmed for me as well.

II

The eighteen years since Henrietta's death in 1983 have brought me more directly to some of the questions I was beginning to ask, or was afraid of asking, when we first met. Our 1979 dinner together, which I thought of at the time as resembling a tea party in a war zone, has come to seem more generally magical and more disturbing. In what way is the life of a cockroach and a human equivalent? Was I, in effect, witnessing a saint embracing creation as the roaches crawled over her, or was I in the presence of a woman whose own paradoxes ("I will not kill roaches, but I will eat fish") demonstrated a fragmentary understanding of some cosmic truth? And what was it, really, that she and I shared about Berry's poem? Was it a poem about love? Perhaps; but the word "love" did not appear in it. Was it a poem about truth? To say such a thing would be to put far too harsh and august a spin on the language of the poem. But if it really was a poem about evanescence and presence, then it was also a poem about the places where language itself cannot go—about a knowing beyond linguistic knowing.

Is this kind of knowing a fantasy? Or is it an essential part of our human reality, a fact of our intuitive being? Certainly some linguists and neurobiologists are increasingly confident about the idea of something like "thought" as independent of language: the neurologist Antonio Damasio speculates about the existence of a "basic neural device" that functions in the body as a "metaself" that is "purely nonverbal"; the linguist Steven Pinker writes (on the subject of freedom as a matter of conception versus a matter of language), "People without a language would still have mentalese...Since mental life goes on independently of particular languages, concepts of freedom and equality will be thinkable even if they are nameless." This idea of a knowing beyond linguistic knowing was something about which Henrietta felt certain; that was clear to me. Interestingly, the same idea was a reasonably decent gloss on Christian Science as well, if any of the editors who had censored the poem had really bothered to think about it.

While Mary Baker Eddy had, in *Science and Health*, various "self-evident truths" and a kind of rough formula for an approach to spiritual healing, it was clear that much wordless understanding—or a wordless, ardent wish for understanding—lay behind those words of hers that strained so much for scientific rigor. And those Christian Scientists who, like the editors, had at times sought healing through prayer also knew that relief comes first, not through language, but through feeling. The problem, finally, was what one might call the epistemology of Berry's poem: a little knowledge, it says, will lead you to ignorance, which will lead you toward the heart of creation. And the last two steps must happen in some way beyond language. That was heresy for Christian Science. But as I have continued my helical movement away from that religion, it has intrigued me to see how a claim for the possibility of knowing beyond language still raises complex problems, even to the point of heresy, for modern cognitive science and paleoanthropology as well. For these disciplines—as even Steven Pinker avers under most circumstances—language defines not only the domain of knowing, but also human nature itself.

"It seems to be fairly generally agreed upon that natural language is indeed uniquely human," writes Michael Corballis in the research journal *Cognition*, citing the work of Bickerton, Chomsky, Kendon, and five other senior researchers in the field of linguistics and cognitive studies. Though until a couple of generations ago, this statement might have seemed ludicrously obvious, more recent research by Penny Patterson, R. L. Holloway, Sue Savage-Rumbaugh, and others has raised the serious possibility of cognitive linguistic skills in animals, particularly (though not exclusively) apes and chimpanzees. Daniel Dennett to some extent refutes this possibility in *Darwin's Dangerous Idea*. Nevertheless, psychologists such as Corballis view language as an evolutionary trait, consistent with the theory of natural selection, and chartable to some degree through evidence of differential brain size between early humanoids.

"The australopithecines [hominids living between 3 and 3.6 million years ago]," writes Corballis, "had brains that were essentially no larger than those of the apes. *H. habilis*, however, had a distinctly larger brain, with an average cranial capacity estimated at 659 cubic centimeters, compared with 451 cubic centimeters for the gracile australopithecines." Citing other research, Corballis notes that "the brain has...virtually tripled in size since the earliest hominids—an increase that is far too great to be attributed to the much less dramatic increase in body size." Equally important, Coballis suggests how the shape of the brain evolved: "There is also evidence from imprints in the cranial cavity that *H. habilis* may have possessed an enlargement on the left side of the brain corresponding to Broca's area."

Corballis' work is interesting in part because he seeks to reconcile the views of paleontologists who argue that language was an unprecedented development, and those of paleontologists who argue that evolutionary theory governs even the rise of language. For Corballis, the possibility that "manual gestures"—a crude sign language—became an early means of hominid communication, shifting to vocal language at about the time that tool use also exploded, suggests an evolutionary development. What is perhaps most striking about this analysis, however (in part because it is not a subject of Corballis' work) is the implicit question of who hominids are at a pre-linguistic, linguistic, and—if this is possible—post-linguistic stage.

I, a writer of essays and poems, exist in a linguistic stage; my nearest paleolithic ancestors, also *Homo sapiens*, may have used both vocal language and tools between 200,000 and 100,000 years ago, according to Corballis, and earlier ancestors—*Homo erectus*, for example, with whom I share an evolutionary line going back perhaps 1.75 million years—may have used some gestural language as well as stone tools. There is an evolutionary break between my line and the next line back, *Homo habilis*, yet even this hominid apparently made and used stone tools between 2.5 and 2 million years ago, and may also have had the capacity for gestural language. It is possible to say that those humans or ape-human creatures, whom we see closely linked yet severed from ourselves, represent a virtually unsolvable question about who we are and—if we believe in notions of spiritual identity—what it is that validates us apart from them. Part of the problem, of course, has to do with how we define language itself, and the kind of cognition related to language. As David Armstrong, William Stokoe, and Sherman Wilcox suggest in *Gesture and the Nature of Language*, "Language has been and always will be gestural"; moreover, "the cognitive structures that underlie language emerge from perceptually guided gestures, prototypically those made by the hands." To the extent that all language arises through the physical reality of the body in relation to the physical reality of the world, language is a phenomenon of the physical creation which reasserts our own biological sources while to some extent denigrating the idea that language somehow emerged of itself, as an evolutionary break, in human brains whose fundamentally different organization resembled nothing else in creation so much as itself. On the other hand, the moment the first hominid made the first gesture, he or she created something entirely new on earth—a story. The gesture that arises as a physical reaction to physical conditions in the environment takes on a life of its own in relation both to the gesturer and to anyone who might perceive and learn to understand the gesture. It is the *story*—the inevitable symbolic corollary of the gesture—that creates the most significant and dangerous distinction on the planet between humans and other species.

In Berry's poem, there are distinctions yet no distinctions: "Being" is something of a trickster figure, a Manhibozo (the trickster figure of Ojibway tribal stories) assuming any incarnation it chooses, yet remaining in some way beyond a particular incarnation. But this does us no good, since we cannot reach that "beyond" without first moving through the specifics of creation and the specifics of our own language to describe that creation. And somewhere in those specifics is a category for a creature quite like and unlike us, called *Australopithecus afarensis* (or "Lucy"), a 3 million-year-old hominid discovered in Ethiopia in 1974 and more recently discovered to have ancestors going back approximately 4.4 million years. Her even more recently-discovered ancestors, *Ardipithecus ramidus kadabba,* alive as many as 5.8 million years ago, evinced in fossil fragments the bipedalism that anthropologists envision as a precursor of gestural language—whether on the African savannahs or in the forests that preceded them. Lucy and her own ancestors are versions of our "being," pre-linguistic, who died to our consciousness until returned in a more-than-spectral form through painstaking scientific research. When we move back toward that version of ourselves, we face the stranger implications of "Being, whose flesh dissolves/ at our glance." And we face the possibility that love fails us as a species.

III

What is love? The question has a Pilate-like ring to it, especially when the value of language itself is in question. But it's fair to ask, especially when one asks about love in relation to intelligence, socialization, and other categories of animal analysis. "Only recently has Western science begun to accept just how sophisticated nonhuman animal behavior can be," write Dale Peterson and Jane Goodall in *Visions of Caliban*, "even in the so-called lower forms of life." But Peterson and Goodall nevertheless warn against a too-liberal application of intelligence to animals:

> For most of us, intelligence implies rational thought, the ability to cope with new situations and solve problems. There is a world of difference in the assassin bug's termite-fishing behavior and that of the chimpanzee. Impressive though the insect's performance may be, it is less flexible, more rigid and preprogrammed, than that of the ape. Which is hardly surprising if we compare the size and complexity of the brains of the two species.

Perhaps one cannot speak in any meaningful way of either intelligence or love among lower species—those which show a very limited ability to adapt and to learn from changes in their environments. Yet one can speak of both intelligence and love—as Goodall and other contemporaries do—among such higher species as apes and chimpanzees. Or at least one can speak of something like love, since the term itself quickly becomes problematic. As Donna Haraway notes in *Primate Visions*, one of the central 20th-century primate experimenters created "mother-machines" for orphaned rhesus monkeys and in other ways stimulated a social feeling that looked like love but might equally have been something else. Still, when Peterson and Goodall describe how a young chimpanzee learns to fish for termites, it's clear that the bond between child and mother is primary.

> We know today that young chimpanzees, like young human children, can learn new behaviors by watching the performances of others, imitating their behavior, and then practicing. At first an infant simply plays around while the mother works—often getting in the way and

having to be pushed gently aside. Then isolated parts of the [mother's] performance appear in the child's growing repertoire of behaviors...

"What intrigues me most about termite fishing," Goodall adds, "is the sense that it is a traditional or cultural behavior." Something is passed along that depends on community, on nurturance and guidance, and these qualities might be said to sound something like "love"—as does, for example, the infant chimpanzee's approach to the more practical task of termite fishing. In "watching," "imitating," and "practicing," the chimpanzee enacts a ritual that looks, not only like a feeding ritual, but equally like a ritual of courtship. The promise of love lies in the practice of feeding: survival gives birth to love.

It could hardly be otherwise, and one only has to look at such "middle" species as cats and dogs, where our language begins to fail us overtly, to see the origins of linguistic confusion. What is a cat or dog doing when she licks her newborn kittens or pups, when she picks them up by the scruff of the neck to bring them all to one place, when she nurses them? Is she "loving" them? Almost any human child would say yes, identifying the animal's behavior with her own mother's or father's. But how is the animal's behavior different from the minimum behavior necessary to ensure the kittens' or pups' survival? Perhaps it is possible to point to a high level of contentment, signaled by purring or deeply rhythmic breathing, which though physiological is not, strictly speaking, necessary: it is something like the pleasure of devotion. But devotion is not love. It is the creature's awareness of the pleasure that ensues because it is doing exactly what it knows it must do. There is, strictly speaking, nothing in the nurturing behavior of a mother dog or cat that implies love.

Yet Penny Patterson sees love in the gorilla Koko's attachment to her pet cat; Jane Goodall sees personal and communal love between chimpanzees; and some paleoanthropologists, such as Donald Johanson, see an evolutionary advance in hominids connected explicitly to bipedalism and implicitly to a shift from devotion to pair-bonding and, perhaps, love. "*Australopithecus afarensis* was probably a social animal," Johanson writes. "Within a larger group, males and females formed monogamous mating pairs and put equal energy into raising offspring." Referring to the theories of his colleague Owen Lovejoy, Johanson adds, "Imposing monogamy upon a large social group is the most novel—and to some critics, unacceptable—aspect of Owen's hypothetical hominid breeding strategy." Even so, Johanson sketches Lovejoy's theory, explaining that bipedalism enabled male hominids in particular to forage for food, carrying it in their arms to female hominids whose devotion to offspring kept them from traveling as far or as fast. (The cultural gender bias in this vision, of course, is something that continues to undergo revision in the work of Adrienne Zihlman, Nancy Tanner, Sarah Mason, and others; women, it now seems clear, were food-gatherers as well. This later research doe not, however, undercut Johanson's essential embrace of bipedalism as a "tool" of cooperation and an incipient route to the brain growth necessary for gestural language.) Whether in some respects Johanson's view also seems alarmingly close to Harry Harlow's "technology of love," as Donna Haraway explains it, it nevertheless serves for Johanson as an evolutionary vision:

> Cooperation increased the odds of males finding food and keeping mates, but certain individuals were better at it than others. Evolution occurs because not everyone succeeds at reproduction and survival. Yet in this network of cooperating, socially interacting hominids...lay the seeds of a later human evolutionary event—the dramatic growth in brain size that marks the emergence of *Homo*. Thus bipedalism could well have been an important catalyst in a novel hominid breeding and survival strategy that incorporated parenting skills, tool use, and other behavior that encouraged brain growth.

In Lovejoy's theory, environmental circumstances and a competition for mates breed a physiological change—bipedalism—which itself makes other behavioral changes possible. Somewhere in this continuum, as the brain grows and becomes more conscious of its consciousness, devotion—the pleasure of doing what one must do—becomes love—the pleasure of knowing oneself transformed through (as Carol Gilligan says) mutual "attention and response."

But having said this, one immediately runs into trouble. Devotion, and perhaps love, center around mating. While it may be excessively capitalistic to suggest that a 3.6 million-year-old hominid possessed his mate, it is clear that Lovejoy attributes notions of success and failure to these sexual encounters *via* evolution: "Evolution occurs because not everyone succeeds at reproduction and survival." If this is true, then the idea of love as a self-transforming relationship based on attention and response becomes oddly narrow and confused, even if it is as shorn as it can be of romantic overtones. For what counts most in a hominid bond—as, perhaps, it still does today—is survival. Survival is predicated, not on a high level of emotional facility, but on an instinctive devotion to one's offspring. To love, then, means to inseminate, to give birth, to take care of, to nurture, to protect from harm, to teach. It means more or less the same for us as it means for Penny Patterson's gorillas or Jane Goodall's chimpanzees. In this way our reproduction and survival are assured.

And yet the largest problem—what we might call spiritual or cultural—remains. Perhaps the most spectacular failure to reproduce or survive is evinced in the life of Jesus, insofar as we know it, and yet for millions of humans he remains the epitome of human love. Moreover, as Denis de Rougement explains, the dimensions of human hope and pleasure which the Church could not, for one reason or another, encode in the figure of Jesus became themselves an alternative vision of love—the courtly love that serves as our model of romance. That early vision still largely defines how we go about seeking our mates, not necessarily for reproduction or survival, but for benediction—for physical and spiritual blessedness. And whether we look toward a religious vision or its competing romantic vision for confirmation of our love, we look where the language of analysis cannot go. We cannot say *what* these loves are, and thus are parted from cognitively meaningful language as effectively as we—or some of us—imagine *Australopithecus afarensis* to have been. But we can tell stories *about* the love that we can neither locate or define, but which invariably locates and defines us.

IV

Love is, above all, a story. When A. N. Wilson refers to Jesus as a "failure," for example, he has created with one word a story of hugely ironic proportions, and that irony resonates with us because we know, or are expected to have learned, that the love Jesus embodied could not have been capable of failure. It is the creation that must have failed, somehow; the love of Jesus was true. What *was* this love? The explanations falter: God, perhaps; or Truth; a compassion that begins and ends in a source beyond humankind. But it is the story, not the level of analysis or the prospective definitions of terms, that makes A. N. Wilson's claim so vibrant. Love is a story.

We thus find ourselves as a species hugely separated from questions of survival. We may die, but our stories will remain; we may all die, but our stories nevertheless will have had an existence apart from us, through our act of creating them. Fleshless, they may "dissolve at our glance," but their temporal presence demonstrates a mode of being beyond the literal. They are our most powerful tool—an unanticipatable extension of the tools of early hominids.

But if love is a story, fundamentally separate from the matter of our physical survival, it is also a kind of lie, a freewheeling gremlin in our human ecosystem, reminding us always that we are not what we seem, and may never be what we seem. People have starved themselves to death for the story of Jesus, and tortured and burned their fellow human beings, and stood by while millions who did not embrace the story were killed. For we, too, have shifted as a species: we no longer imagine our survival as dependent simply on the gathering of food or the warding off of predators. We imagine our survival as based on stories—stories of love and community, of economy and nation, of political and social oppression and release from oppression. It is in story-telling, the act of language, that we separate ourselves from the rest of creation. And yet, at some ultimate level, we tell stories of a connectedness that language itself may have robbed from us.

If you are skilled in the art of meditation, for example, you may begin with a story—a bit of language, a mantra—and keep that language before you until it ceases to become language, until it ceases to become anything at all, and in its nothingness the something that is nothing becomes apparent to you, and the calm that descends is intensely unifying—animal, spiritual, without distinction or name. How do you communicate such an experience to others? And where do you locate its source? In a personal soul? In a deity? In a physiological reaction to a state of extreme mental calm? None of these is sufficient, nor is the language used to describe them. Such a person provokes us to two choices—on the one hand an increasing reliance on the explanations of biochemistry, which substitutes chemical formulae for the experience of blessedness; and on the other, an increasing reliance on a kind of skilled silence to convey something at once immanent and apart from normal human experience.

Does love lie in either of these zones? I doubt it. Both of them are beyond love—the first by virtue of its discipline, its mathematical and symbolic language, and its categories; the second by virtue of its beautifully consuming emptiness. Perhaps more important, both of these have no story to tell. Although dramatic stories of scientific discovery are rooted in our culture, there is, strictly speaking, no narrative in chemical compounds—or, for that matter, in meditative insight. The story that is love lies elsewhere—perhaps pointing toward one or the other of these ends, but perhaps pointing in a completely different way, and implying a completely different experience for those who encounter it. By virtue of being a story, it cannot be an ultimate, an end. It must always be imperfect, partial. In this lies its great danger.

V

A story presupposes certain elements—there is a man, say, or a woman, or a child, and these people will be transformed in some way through their experience of specific events. This means, of course, that story is fundamentally psychological. But what connection does that psychological dimension have with the creature we imagine ourselves to be? If one looks to theorists of the brain for possible answers, it would seem that we betray ourselves with stories. "The brain is a biological organ with biological functions," writes Noel Smith in the research journal *The Psychological Record*. Observations about how humans behave when, for example, parts of their brains are damaged "do not support the assumption that it is a psychological organ: There is no man inside the man, no woman inside the woman; the brain does not direct or control behavior." Smith views the brain as a "strictly biological coordinating organ that functions in interdependence with other biological components. The more complex the brain the more complex the remainder of the organism with which it is integrated and in turn the more complex the behavior that is enabled to develop."

But a story is not biological. It *is* "a man inside the man,...[a] woman inside the woman." Thus it would seem that we betray our biological identities with stories. But do we transcend those identities as well?

The notion of "transcendence" is itself a story which suggests that, as consciousness meditates on itself, it becomes other than the biological entity which gives it a context. We (or I) cannot bear to be non-psychological, non-spiritual, or organic in the most literal sense; what we tell ourselves about love confirms the possibility that we may be liberated from this unbearable burden. In seeking, and finding, another human who reflects or extends our own desire to be known, cherished, and released from the most deadening mechanisms of our daily life and culture, we find what seems a center—a place of comfort where our stories come to rest, where language need not go, where all is understood. Is this romantic fantasy? Perhaps—except that many people experience such an event at least once in their lives, and that event transforms them. If this event comes to a premature close—if, for example, a love affair fails—they may yearn so ardently for its return that, finally, another human being may be insufficient to provide it. Thrust back into the fact of their biological origin by the exigencies and limitations of the relationship, they see that an individual story of love has failed—failed to carry them further out of their "loneliness and partiality," as Ezra Pound said, failed to carry them further into that zone of comfort—and yet they have experienced, and thus believe in, its reality.

If these people then spend the rest of their lives looking for what they have lost, as the speaker of William Butler Yeats' "Song of Wandering Aengus" does, they are speaking to the abject failure of a particular story of love, even as they glorify the larger, impersonal story. "Though lovers be lost love shall not," writes Dylan Thomas, "And death shall have no dominion." These stories we tell ourselves, which appeared at some point to have so little to do with our physical survival, now draw from us a form of faith that assures *their* survival: they have, effectively, a life of their own, quasi-biological though without embodiment, as if we had created a symbiosis in which one creature is always sub-microscopic, a shadow, a ghost. And this ghost promises us that some things will not die; that love will not die; that death shall not triumph. The man behind the man and woman behind the woman in such stories may be tragic figures, but—because of their essential presence—they will at some point be synonymous with redemption.

Given such a story about transcendence, about the temporal and the enduring, it might be well to wish for the opposite, in which there is no man behind the man, no woman behind the woman. One wants to withdraw one's consent from a story which makes us so profoundly psychological, so available to emotional damage, so questing, so unfulfilled. A story of lifelong unfulfillment in service to a higher reality is, after all, a story of species failure—a failure of the species to live as itself in the creation in which it finds itself. And that is a very dangerous story indeed.

But that is the story we tell ourselves endlessly. And because it is a story we feel in common with other primates—with grieving female gorillas, for example, who have lost their young, or with baby rhesus monkeys driven to obvious madness through experimental isolation and the false comfort of a "mother-machine"—we know that it exists in some way at a pre-linguistic level. It is a story we must have shared with our hominid ancestors, a story older than *Homo habilis*, a story far older than human language. It is, perhaps, our first tool. And in that act of archaic craftsmanship, we begin to re-define ourselves, to evolve. The evolution of hominids, which is so often theorized as depending on bipedalism and tool use and brain size, may as well have been encouraged by the emotions of grief and loss for which there was no controlling force, nothing but a pre-linguistic story that had, finally, to find its expression.

But if, as linguistic hominids, we have refined the story of grief and loss into the story of love and redemption, there remains the question of what this "love" is. Perhaps it is, as I suggested earlier, the pleasure of knowing oneself transformed through... "attention and response." But perhaps it is something different—a statement, rooted in biology, of our fearful inadequacy as a species against the powers of nature, and a plea for some recognition, from somewhere, other than that which comes to us from the natural environment. King Lear, raging on the heath, may be mad, but he indicts human biology and the crushing weight of nature by his presence, and we see the necessity of a story of love in his very loss of that story. Something must save us. And yet, curiously, humans since the late Pleistocene, and perhaps before, had as part of their biological make-up the capacity to imagine or enter states of consciousness which make the physical world seem to them other than it ordinarily seems.

The impetus of such a peculiar religion as Christian Science, after all, is that the physical world—itself ultimately unreal—can be transformed through a profound understanding of that imagined place in which there is no man behind the man, no woman behind the woman. This requires a reader to understand these terms in exactly the opposite way from the way in which Noel Smith uses them, for in Christian Science the limits and authority of physical creation no longer exist. This act of faith is by no means idiosyncratic, whatever the idiosyncracies of that particular religion. Recent historians of Jesus, for example, such as A. N. Wilson and Geza Vermes (in his meticulously-documented *Jesus the Jew*), argue for Jesus' closeness to the early Hasidim, whose confidence in spiritual healing—that is, transforming certain conditions of the physical world through a faith in the ultimate power of spirit to bring the physical world into congruence with it—was an unquestionable part of their religious observance. Vermes writes:

That a distinctive trend of charismatic Judaism existed during the last couple of centuries of the Second Temple is undeniable. These holy men were treated as the willing or unsuspecting heirs to an ancient prophetic tradition. Their supernatural powers were attributed to their immediate relation to God. They were venerated as a link between heaven and earth independent of any institutional mediation.

In some ways—although the Hasidim emphasized the power of holy speech, and although in the Christian tradition John averred the primacy of the Word—this healing tradition is a post-linguistic human development. It presumes the kind of evolutionary break in a story that Stephen Jay Gould envisions in the evolutionary fossil record: suddenly an event occurs, and the old story vanishes; a new story appears. But in that time of vanishing—whether the time is infinitesimal or long—there is some deed without or apart from language. An event occurs that we cannot describe. And yet its presence does not signal our annihilation. On the contrary, those who have experienced something they would describe as spiritual healing describe themselves as more fully *themselves*, more truly alive, and—most important—more removed from whatever dimensions of the previous story of their lives oppressed them. It is urgent to understand that, at a moment of profound change—whether it occurs in our lives or in our witnessing of life across the history of the planet—the reality of the event is post-linguistic. It is not accessible to the story. "One thing I know," says the blind man whom Jesus healed, "that, whereas I was blind, now I see." This is not the story people want; they can see the miracle; but they want the story *of* the miracle. But that is not a story. That is something else.

Whatever that something else is, it partakes of a level of reality that we know to be central to our being. We do not, as a species, reach that level very often. Perhaps what is most discouraging about the stories of love that we tell ourselves is that these stories can lead us to the threshold of that reality—can, in certain cases, lead us across the threshold—but, being creatures of language at this evolutionary juncture, we do not know how to explain or trust the reality we are being given. There is always that other world we inhabit—the world of explanations, commitments, other relationships, and concepts of obligation, betrayal, normality—which is, effectively, our home. It is a world of language, of love and failed love, of a modicum of comfort, of dismay, of tragedy. We are comfortable there, miserably comfortable as it may turn out, even unto death. Curiously, this zone of language, behavior, and feeling may *appear* to be the equivalent, for humans, of a "home range," explaining in part why contemporary humans still seem to find so little kinship with their environment, and why they continue to find it perfectly normal both to cause grievous harm to this environment and to move regularly around the country in search of a better (or adequate) job, a better relationship, a better something. And even if this "zone" of a linguistically-dominated reality is a far cry from a true home range, its power as an illusion further raises the question of how language removes us from a necessarily bodily reality—a necessary comfort, a certainty, a center.

Interestingly, that feeling of comfort and centeredness may arrive within a zone of post-linguistic knowing in which stories end: we *feel* what we always thought we might feel but could never explain. Can we live there? Can we survive there? Only if we jettison that one quality which makes us most human—our story-telling—or, perhaps more miraculously, learn to commute between those two zones—the one timelessly comforting, the other trapped in time and sadness and happiness. Such commuting between two "home ranges," neither of which has a clear anchor in this world, creates the ghost man. For those who embrace the story of Christianity, this was the role of Jesus, and if his fate is seen as a failure, it is a failure which indicts most of all the stories that bear his name. The story of the morning of the third day, for example, when Mary goes to the sepulchre to find Jesus and finds only the place where he lay, is a story of an absence. And for those who believe, Jesus' reappearances after this absence suggest that what is at the heart of our evolutionary lives is an empty tomb, beyond which whatever it is we call love operates according to rules we cannot name.

It is strange, then, to consider what pre-linguistic and post-linguistic creation may have in common. My old friend and colleague Henrietta cherished animals because they had "souls"—which, perhaps, to her, meant that they were linked to her own livelihood through versions of feeling, realities which finally eluded language. It was necessary, to her, to find the reality that lay beyond language, if only to witness how humans were fundamentally separate from the identities they created for themselves through the telling of stories. Because they did not tell stories, animals could be closer to this reality than humans—closer by virtue of something I have called feeling, but which might exist even at the lowest level as a kind of necessity of being absolutely what one is—cat, rat, lizard, scorpion, or cockroach. And yet, having learned to be separate from this creaturely imperative, this "Being" in Berry's poem, humans were wedded to stories as their imperfect evolutionary way of returning to a place of certainty where stories vanished—where "the darkness keeps us near you." And because the stories vanished, this darkness was also light, and nearness was vast distance, and love and not-love were immanent: and then all words fled.

It is possible, still, to be frightened of evolutionary theory, and to see in the evidence of our hominid ancestors the absence of God—for who could have created so marginal a species for the largely mechanistic pleasure of watching it grow into something more dexterous, more manipulative, and vastly more powerful? But this fear, as Henrietta knew, I think, misrepresents the sources of human power. To *Australopithecus afarensis,* walking the African savannah, or to *Ardipithecus ramidus kadabba,* desperately alert for predators in the African tropical forests 5.8 million years ago, power could not have been separate from a feeling of terror on the one hand, and a sensibility—a straightening up toward the sun—of all being exactly as it was. This sensibility, a kind of devotion, was made different by the constant nearness of terror—an equal sensibility of things not being as they should be or, much later, could be—and in this split, at first biologically based, grew a consciousness of division and grief and loss.

This consciousness, which ultimately became the vehicle of story, was also a consciousness that became increasingly unaware of the authority of its own being. Yet it had known that once, as a cat knows it, as a one-celled creature "knows" its DNA; if one believes Antonio Damasio, that "nonverbal metaself" exists still, inescapably, in the human body. Somewhere, in the evoution of consciousness, words replaced wordlessness, but the sense of a home beyond words never vanished. And now, as we begin to suspect that consciousness is in some way separate from the biology of its human context, we nevertheless see that in meditating on itself it must ultimately silence itself, and in that silence find the being that is the source and end of all life.

If I have reached the fringes of that awareness, it does not, I think, mean that I am somehow closer to a redemptive reality than I might otherwise have been. Like the blind man who was healed, I know what I have not seen and what I have seen, and what I have seen makes me painfully aware of how much I still rely on the power of stories, particularly stories of love. If I can never resolve, never move beyond, the story that gave birth to this book, for example—a story of dwindling love, of new love, of an incipient transformation that, for unchartable reasons, could not be completed—then perhaps I will have demonstrated, more than anything else, how I remained trapped in my own stories, and how, evolutionarily speaking, I remain the prey of the tool my ancestors used to bring me here. And so I must trust, as most people still do, in the power of stories to lead where there are no words, and hope that, as inexplicable as that may be, it will yield the feelings that transform the world into a domain where love is primal—if only we could call it nothing, and not "love."

Hasidim: A Seventeen-Year Postscript

Yes, I know: I live a great deal inside my own head.
I ask questions that cannot be answered, though I expect answers.
I contradict myself.
Last night I dreamed I was walking down a rather run-down street in a small northern city—the kind I often imagine myself living in—and saw two grizzly bears a couple of blocks away, snarling and batting each other on the sidewalk. I skirted the animals by going down an alley, yet always they were in sight. I knew that I should be afraid of them, which is why I went around them, but I was not afraid of them. It shocked me, a few minutes later, to find that the police had already been called and had already captured one of the bears. The other had escaped. But to where? (Not until years later would I read, in Carlos Castaneda's *Tales of Power*, the story of the two cats—one who assents to his capture and death, and the other who must escape—as the bear in my dream escaped—as I was supposed to escape. "To where" was not important; the point was *to live*.)

But what good is it to believe in the power of a bear, or of a remote northern village, if I live so much inside my head? What is it that makes a transformation of one's life more than an escape? I write about others, about myself, about the world, about bears, about guns, about primates and humans, about love, and look toward the day when I will no longer write. But will I cease to be, then? Would that be bad?

"Who are you, and what do you love?"

These questions return insistently, even though I have dismissed their value in comparison to Job-like questions of outrage.

I contradict myself.

Some pages ago, I said that everything has a language. More recently, I said that language is an intermediate state in our development; that we know that meaning exists beyond language; and that we must somehow reach this level of meaning to understand something essential about our being. How can "everything have a language" if language is merely an evolutionary stage?

Perhaps what I meant to say was that, for us, now, everything has a language; but much of that "language" is not verbal, and its generative grammar shapes in us a form of awareness we can feel but not speak. This is the language of recognition, of being recognized. But what does that mean?

I will tell you a story.

II

Three days before our cat died, he woke me from a dreamless sleep. The moon at 3 A.M. was full, and shone through the window with a pale resonance. I awoke to find two bright black eyes staring at me. Although this had happened to me once when I was a year old, still in a crib, and ever after I had always had a fear of animals attacking me in the middle of the night, for some reason I was not startled this time. It may have been because the cat had been mewing a few moments earlier, and although I was not conscious of being awake I may have heard the sound. As we stared at each other, I realized that he wanted something.

But what? He was eating virtually nothing; the vet had told us earlier in the day that both of his kidneys were virtually dead, and that his liver was failing as well. When he wanted to be petted, he usually stuck his head under my hand, but he had not done that this time. No; I did not know what he wanted. We stared at each other. Although I did pet him, he seemed not to notice. Like most cats, he had an expressive face, which allowed me to attribute various emotions to him if I was willing, but I had never seen this expression before.

He wanted to look into my eyes. It was strange, but that was what he did, sitting there on my chest, purring, staring. I looked back. We did this for a minute or two; then he turned away, settling at the other end of the bed.

I was sad. I felt that he knew he was dying, and wanted me to help him, but I could not. He was asking me for his life, and I could not give it to him. Sleeping fitfully for the rest of the night, I awoke in a low mood. "I'm not an animal," I said to myself without thinking. That was what I had been raised to believe, and it was virtually a rote response whenever the subject came up.

But then I saw: I was an animal to our cat, who identified me that way because he knew that's what I was. *He* recognized me as an animal; *he* saw it in *my* stare. Whatever was tormenting him, he sought something he recognized, some creature who could recognize him—the stare of knowing. "I know what you are," we said as we stared, although I did not know I was saying this and could not really explain what it meant. No language entered into it; it was simply mutual recognition.

The cat was nowhere to be found the next day, when I had to leave on a 2,000-mile drive to Seattle. I was grieved to leave, because I felt certain I would not see him again, but I could not find him to say good-bye. Two days later, in a motel in Billings, Montana, I called Lesley to find that she had had the cat put to sleep. His suffering had grown too obvious, incurable. The vet estimated his age at 16 or 17 years, older than we had thought; we had found him as a stray in California in October 1985. He had been a dear companion.

Though I was both grateful to Lesley and sad for her, it was much more difficult to explain my own feelings. I felt, on the one hand, as if yet another death in my life had happened apart from me; once again, it had been a distant, silent affair. Yet I kept the feeling of this cat's presence close within me. While I was not denying his death, something particular had not died. I realized, as I drove down Interstate 90 toward Seattle, that what endured was his gaze. He had known who I was.

III

I will tell you another story.

In June 1984, I went for the first time to Jerusalem. Although the dirt and chaos and richness of the Old City startled me (I had never before been greeted by a goat shitting at the entrance to a city), I was stunned by the Temple Mount, and by the long, high expanse of the Western Wall. Few people were praying there when I arrived on a weekday morning. As my wife and our friend Jennie prepared to go down to the women's side of the wall, I made my way to the men's side. I wanted very much to touch it although, having relatively little connection with Judaism, I could not say why.

As I descended the stairs to the wall, I felt myself descending in time, growing older with indescribable speed until, as I approached the wall itself, I felt enormously heavy—a compressed presence, like a magical ball, full of light but also of horror. I stayed some inches from the wall at first. A soldier in fatigues and a yarmulke was praying aloud to my left; to my right, across the partition separating male and female worshippers, a woman in a black shawl bowed her head until it touched the stone. I felt for a moment as if I could go through the wall. What stopped me were the bits of paper, hundreds and hundreds of small pieces, prayers, crammed into the crevices of the rock. I reached to touch one of the rocks that held the prayers, and stayed in that position for awhile. Although I knew many prayers from my religion, I said none of them, waiting for one to materialize in my head. But none did.

Then, glancing to the left, past the soldier, I saw a small group of orthodox Jews in a grotto under the main approach to the Temple Mount. Even before I made eye contact with them, they were beckoning to me, waving me over. Impossible; they must want the soldier. But they were not looking at the soldier; they were looking at me. The soldier finished his prayer, kissed his shawl, and departed. The bearded, black-garbed men at the grotto entrance were beckoning to me.

Blonde, blue-eyed, slight, dressed in Sportif shorts and my usual long-sleeved shirt and bush hat, I could scarcely have looked more like an American tourist. And who knows what they really wanted? Perhaps they wanted to scold me for touching the wall. Perhaps they wanted to assail me for my irreverent dress, to send me away; perhaps they wanted to convert me. All of these crossed my mind, as I stood with my left fingers still on the stone of the Western Wall, but I did not believe any of them. What I saw in their eyes was recognition.

Whatever their own frailties, they believed themselves to be children of God, and trusted in the reality of a divinely-authorized world. And they saw that I, too, was of that world—even though, at the time, I was in the full regalia of doubt, and had come to Israel in part to see if anything other than doubt could really inhabit my life.

We stared at each other for several seconds—they looking and beckoning intently, not hostile but passionate; I standing with my hand on the wall. And then I bowed to them, and shook my head, and walked away.

The "real" meaning of this I cannot say. I do not even know for certain they were Hasidim, although when I looked at them I felt my own jolt of recognition as the word "healing" ran through my mind; later, looking up various Jewish sects in the library, it was the Hasidim who came closest to my imagined contact with the men in the Old City. Whoever they were, I knew that, even as I could not become one of them, they had sensed that we shared a common reality. I knew who they were; they knew who I was.

IV

It strikes me that very few people in the world actually know each other. Most of us have many acquaintances, a few friends. On a gloomy day, it's easy to believe that most of the people we pass on the street do not know and, for that matter, do not care who we are, as we—perhaps—do not care who they are. Often we are more than wrapped in our own cares. We live in a world of care, a world of hurt. Our colleagues, worried about their workloads or job prospects or families or lack of family, are so uncentered and scattered that it is difficult to find the time or place to reach beyond those cares to something more enduring— if, indeed, there is anything more enduring. Our friends, even good friends, come and go...it's a transient world. I had wonderful friends in high school in California, for example, but now they are all scattered; a number are dead— drownings, cancer, suicide. Only three high school friends that I know of still live in the West; we hear from each other perhaps once a year, once every five years, or not at all. We are pulled in a thousand different directions, starting our lives over and over, adding to them in the hope of finding something essential about ourselves, of doing some essential good for the world...and then confusion sets in, and weariness, and we wonder how it is that we managed to travel so far along the same uncharted routes our parents and their parents seem to have taken.

And yet we crave recognition (though not, I think, the kind Francis Fukuyama discusses in his once-prominent *The End of History*). Above all, it seems, we want someone to be able to say "I know who you are" and mean it. It doesn't have to be a person; it can be an animal, which is partly why some people become more attached to their pets than to any other human being, and why pet cemeteries, as ludicrous as they may seem to the uninitiated, mean a great deal to those who bury their companions there. "This animal," they are saying implicitly, "knew me; no one else did." If that seems tragically sad, it is no sadder than most of what we live through in the vast circus of western culture.

To be recognized this way, apart from language, at some instinctive level of knowing, is to enter into the non-narrative of love, the love even deeper than the stories of love that we think of as, in part, defining our humanity. I, for example, do not want to be seduced, to be whisked to a romantic hideaway, to spend enormous sums of money on sumptuous cruises and hotels and thus impress my erotically-inflamed date. I want to be known. And while many people invest great sums of money in elegant erotic play, I would wager that they, too, want most of all to be recognized—the more so if they, for whatever reason, cannot recognize themselves.

I look at myself in the mirror: who am I? The face stares back opaquely—sometimes, I think, a little on the scarred-handsome side, at other times irresolute and cowardly, sometimes my father's face, sometimes a face I have never seen in any photographs in any albums of any of my extended family going back four generations. I do not recognize myself. In fact, if I can bring myself to stare as honestly as I stared at my dying cat, or at the Hasidim in Jerusalem, I find I have almost never recognized myself. Perhaps there is an element of self-loathing here, such as one finds in many humans, despite their reluctance to admit it. But I also think there's an element of basic confusion. I see myself in the eyes of an animal, and I am an animal; I see myself in the eyes of charismatic Jews, and I am a charismatic Jew. How can these be conjoined? Yet, in my life, they are somehow conjoined, and if I were truly attentive to myself I should be able to take comfort in that fact.

But I am always running from it, or almost always—too wedded, still, to the idea that life is purely "spiritual," knowing that, in a species on the verge of post-linguistic knowledge, that world means less than nothing, yet using it to say, "I am not of this world, I cannot be of this world." The home range, wherever it might be, recedes. This reflex is part of the way I do not recognize myself; I disguise myself in the religious language of my childhood, and fade before my eyes as quickly as my reflection vanishes when I flip off the light.

Unable to trust the motions of my heart, which were damaged so early by language, I look outward into the world for confirmation of who I am; from time to time, I find it. And as I found it once in Jerusalem, and once in my own bedroom, with a dying cat, I also found it once or twice in love. I felt myself cherished and transformed; the story of romantic love, which itself is finite and has origins in a split between religious culture and secular culture in the Middle Ages, was nevertheless my saving story. But when a love struck that was not, fundamentally, romantic—when I looked into another's eyes and saw there her recognition of me, which put at risk everything I had invested myself in to that point—I saw again how mercilessly honest this experience of recognition can be,

Thomas Simmons

and how, in some ways, it may not be of this world. It does not, after all, recognize the world's limits. The woman who recognized me knew, as quickly as I, the dangers we were headed toward; the cat who recognized me knew his death was near; the Hasidim in Jerusalem knew I would have to die to my old life, and knew, the moment I released my hand from the Western Wall, that I could not do that—at least not with them.

But when life is long, as mine appears to be, one inevitably begins to ask: what is the pattern here? What is it that a few creatures and humans have seen, and how is it that I have recognized their recognition? What does that tell me about myself? Will I be false to some emergent self unless I turn from the life I am now living, even as I write these words, and vanish into a world where I am recognized, however foreign that may appear? Or can I perform this act of recognition for myself?

To me, that vanishing still sounds too close to the principle of the cult, a final surrender of something that never was meant to be surrendered. I find myself hoping, then, that the miracle of mutual recognition comes down to something even more private, in which the self alone says to itself, "They have known you, and you have known the you that they have known; that is the you whom God knows." Although that sentence may sound like pseudo-poetic nonsense, it is not. And it makes possible—perhaps—a zone of aloneness, *place,* where one can love oneself and the world without feeling the terror of utter isolation. It makes possible a home range. Once again the helix triumphs: we go down into those selves which others knew to be ours to find that place beyond language where we can begin to shape for ourselves a new story of love. And no matter what our future holds, we must for the time being have that story—because we are human, because we are animal, because we are of God, and because, all too rarely, we are known.

Epilogue

*It sounds like care: querencia—and it means
affection or fondness, coming from* querer,
*to want or desire or love, but also to accept
a challenge as in a game, but also it means
a place chosen by a man or animal—querencia—
the place one cares most about, where one is
most secure, protected, where one feels safest.*

—Stephen Dobyns

    I returned to Anchorage in early autumn. Out of the darkness, as we descended above the Chugach mountains, the basin of Anchorage shimmered in the translucent overcast, half of Alaska's population announcing its presence with a modern equivalent of oil-lamp light, a sign of welcome. Nevertheless, I could not help feeling sad the next morning, awakening to a coldness as sharp as Iowa's but in light much more pale, almost like a luminous mist rising up to water the face of the earth. What might this have been, what place might this have been... But that was a long time ago. "Dreams die hard," David Harris once wrote, but they do die.

    Still I went to Merrill Field later that day—Merrill is one of five airports in the immediate vicinity of Anchorage—and had myself certified at Flight Safety Alaska (later known as Take Flight Alaska) to fly a Cessna 172 (I had earned a pilot's license some years ago, had a current medical certificate, and needed only to show my logbook and demonstrate my competency as a 172 pilot to be able to rent a plane during daylight hours). The flight checkride in and out of Merrill is a test of basic skills, memory, and nerves, because to fly out of Merrill one must either fly lower than 600 feet or higher than 2,000 (the space in between is reserved for other planes going in and out of other airports). At peak hours Merrill Field alone has 150 to 200 of what the FAA calls "movements" (takeoffs and landings). Because climbing to more than 2,000 feet in a Cessna in the Merrill area requires a very specific route either over City High School or over West High School, some people elect what's called the Ship Creek departure: this takes you across Knik Arm, with its 43-degree water, at an altitude of 500 feet, so that if you lose the engine you are faced with almost-certain death, but it's the only completely straightforward departure from Merrill, and thus a tempting one.

Thomas Simmons

I brought the plane up to 500 feet, leveled off, and shot out over the dark water of Knik Arm. My flight instructor that day, a man who had moved to Alaska from Connecticut eight years earlier because of a divorce, said little, but what he said registered: "You know, at 500 feet, if your engine quits, you don't have much of a chance down there," he said. "Might want to try a different departure next time." Though I was out of practice and somewhat clumsy with the plane—not beautifully smooth as I once had been—it was a routine checkride, and I passed the test. The next day I took the rented Cessna and went north, toward Talkeetna and beyond, to one of America's holy places, Denali.

It had begun to occur to me that I had taken up flying, back in 1990, because so many things seemed in flux—not only in my professional life at MIT, where I then taught, and in my marriage, where my wife and I seemed locked in a battle of passive mutual destruction, but in my thinking about place and love and story. Perhaps the place of humans could change radically and rightfully, I began to think, and perhaps love really could be a season in the air, and the experience of love might happen beyond words in a zone of meaningful abstractions: compass headings, altitudes, angles of attack. On the whole, of course, I was wrong; life in the air had terrible limits and costs. But *in the air,* life was sweet; I remembered that; I had missed it.

Climbing to 4,500 feet out of the Anchorage basin, heading northwest to Talkeetna, I realized the immensity of my forgetfulness. There was no land I knew of in the lower 48 like this. Though I roughly followed the Susitna River, with its black water and pools of ice and snow, I had forgotten the hundreds of tributaries and the plains around them, and the forests beyond them, forests of such depth and width and poverty and excess that no human could or would have planned such things, forests that seemed to clump together for miles or clear suddenly in a semi-swampy mess of land. There was no human measure here. It was all a divine desolation. How would I live, I wondered over the roar of the engine, if this *were* my home range, if one of my dreams had come true? How hard it would be, how hard the simplest things would be—as everyone who came seriously to the Alaskan country knew. Here I might become an intelligent animal in its quest for food, for shelter, for solitude or companionship. Here, in the darkness of the winter days or the spring afternoons and nights, those ideas that might come to me after the labor of surviving might not be in words like these, but rather in feelings—how should I say it?—feelings of realities that conjoined this one, and affirmed this one, yet offered alternatives. It was a strange thought, as I looked past the forest to the mountains of the Alaska range, where I would be as soon as I refueled in Talkeetna. So much about this trip was *not* about words, or even—I find this hard to say—about loss.

II

A while back, in late February 1998, I made my way from Iowa City to San Francisco for a combined conference and workshop that I could hardly have regarded more skeptically. Michael Harner, for some years a professor of anthropology and more recently a shamanistic practitioner and researcher in his own right, was offering a "basic" course on shamanic practice, and I, who had come to the history—and the controversy—of shamanism very slowly over the past decade, decided that, regardless of doubt, I should attend. There are some things one finds one cannot give up, despite years of misery and disillusionment, and one such unrelinquishable force for me was spiritual healing: as a Christian Science child, I had the idea of spiritual healing bred into me before I could even speak, and though, as far as I knew, it had mostly failed me—had always failed me in matters of the body—I could not let go of the idea that something often happened in the human body and psyche that neither language nor medicine could account for, and that people who were serious about such things owed it to themselves not to give up.

Trying to save money where I could, I checked into a slightly shabby two-story motel in the SoMa (South of Market) district of San Francisco, making my way the next morning to the shining campus of the University of San Francisco, where Harner and his associates from the Foundation for Shamanic Studies were convening the weekend gathering. Of the 130 or so people there, about 110 struck me immediately as frightening—no doubt a consequence, in part, of my white-shirt-and-starched-trousers upbringing, but also a consequence of their longing: the many people were dressed in a kind of NewAge-American Indian-Banana Republic garb, with beads and rattles and drums and wool blankets from various Indian tribes. I felt as if I had walked into precisely what scholar Alice Kehoe criticized in an issue of the *American Indian Quarterly* a year before when she went after the dangerous ambiguities of this kind of practice.

For the first half-hour of the workshop—as Michael Harner led, first a prayer, then a chanting and drumming (and howling) session—I held the underside of my chair with my hands and said, "I am here for a reason, and I am not leaving, no matter how horrible these people are." Later that day, Harner got off one of the funniest lines I have ever heard from a speaker to his audience: "I know why you're all here," he said near the end of the afternoon. "You're here because psychotherapy failed you, and you're all desperate." The few of us who laughed gathered some ugly stares from the large number of people who didn't.

I was there because, like many people, I had read Mircea Eliade's *Shamanism: Archaic Techniques of Ecstasy,* and while I had no idea in 1995 (when I first encountered it) how little field work Eliade had done or how suspect some of his sources were, I recognized details of my childhood—illnesses, depressions, a sense of being led to or toward a vision during a time of crisis. I wondered whether, across human history and culture, there had been evidence of spiritual power that could touch even me, a failed child of the late 20th century. My interest grew as I read, a bit later, the Russian psychiatrist Olga Kharitidi's book on Siberian shamanism, and some anthropological studies of contemporary shamanic practice in Indonesia: the lines of connection, though shaky in places, were also compelling in others, and felt, again, familiar. When, in Harold Bloom's *Omens of Millennium*, I read his brief account of Jesus as a shaman, the route was set: I had to know whether there was a power available to me like the power I had been promised as a child in Christian Science. I had to know whether I might relearn my identity as a ghost man by finding a spiritual practice that kept me clearly rooted in this world—in a home range of my heart—while offering me the consolations, insights, and powers of "another" world. Such a practice might, I thought, make up for the lost dreams of love, of retreat, in Alaska or the Cascades...such a practice might bring a ghost man back to life.

For true spiritual practitioners there are no accidents, but I accidentally stumbled on the website of the Foundation for Shamanic Studies while playing with my office computer in the early fall of 1997. In a few weeks, I had a newsletter, a list of conferences, workshops, and training sessions (one of which lasted three years)—and, perhaps most comically from certain points of view, a CD (a CD!) of "shamanic drumming." The four tracks made it possible to attempt to experience a shamanic trance in a fifteen to thirty-minute period with single or double drumming. The four colleagues to whom I confided this new experiment did not, amazingly, laugh (though one might expect they had given up laughing at me a long time ago); one, in fact, the one who seemed the most temperamentally skeptical, was actually profoundly interested, which brought me some comfort. But the real test was simply to devote myself to the drums and the darkness and the events that followed. Thus one evening, late, after it seemed likely that no one could think of anything to call me about, I turned out all the lights, meditated on a question I wished a guardian animal from the Lower World to help me answer, and played the drums on my CD player.

I doubted anything would happen, yet something did. It was interesting enough, and in some ways consoling enough, that I wrote it down; I wrote down several other similar experiments as well that I conducted over the next several weeks. By then I had read, not only various scholarly studies on shamanism (and some current critiques of western hybridizations of specific shamanic practices from different cultures), but also Michael Harner's *The Way of the Shaman* (which is—to some people's delight or outrage—a classic distillation of many cultures' experience with shamanic journeying to the Lower World, a real but generally inaccessible world that parallels our own and from which and to which our spirits periodically travel, with or without our consent). I had also read his colleague Sandra Ingerman's *Soul Retrieval*, a book of "practical" shamanism for people who had suffered a "soul loss" as a result of some terrible accident or event. In certain ways, these books were both about trauma and awakening from trauma, another subject I had been studying intensively: it was Cathy Caruth's *Unclaimed Experience* that helped me to see the paradox that to awaken from a trauma did not always mean to *know* it, and there was much to which I had awakened that I neither knew nor understood. Now, however, as I "journeyed" shamanically, people and events and destinations came into view in a way that began to re-shape some of my loneliness and my yearning. Unfortunately, the answers were often so overwhelming—and so inexplicable even to sympathetic others—that I felt at a loss about what to do next. That loss brought me to Harner in San Francisco.

Once the workshop got underway, once the drumming and howling hordes quieted down and Harner gave instructions for specific kinds of shamanic journeys, I felt better. The audience broke into pairs, assisting each other in their initiatory practice, and I felt happy with the woman I worked with—someone sitting next to me who, indeed feeling desperate about her life, had heard about the workshop the day before and had simply walked in that morning, a relatively unheard-of practice for a Harner workshop. She was thoughtful and funny and sweet; her desperation felt familiar; we worked well together. As we compared notes about what we had asked for and what we had seen, I felt understood (though we each had to try not to giggle about what we were doing and how it might have looked, say, to our respective relatives); she seemed to feel the same. The usual wariness of wounded older single people kept us from having lunch together or dinner later, and—as these things go—that proved to be a disastrous wariness; but I did not know that at the time. Despite my anxieties about the tenor of the workshop and most of the participants, I came back for the afternoon session with some sense that I was home. I could know here, and be known.

In the afternoon, Harner did something extraordinary for a first-day group: he had us conduct, or attempt to conduct, a shamanic healing for another member of the audience. We switched partners; I was paired with a young man, perhaps 15 years younger than I, who looked, I had to admit, as if he had spent the past decade living in a northern California forest (a prospect which, at that moment, sounded fine to me). We each asked, by way of healing, for some kind of vision in relation to romance. I wanted to know what had happened to the woman who had said to me, "You're the man I'm supposed to meet," and he wanted to know what had happened to a woman who had recently dumped him after an intense and seemingly flourishing three-month affair. The lights dimmed; Harner and his assistant drummed quietly, four beats a second, for fifteen minutes; the huge room otherwise was silent.

After a few minutes of darkness, time in my mind seemed to compress, and much happened quickly: the hawk who had been my guide brought me through the darkness to a high plateau, where a young woman sat facing the dawn. Though the young man I was working with had not described the woman to me, the woman I saw had quite specific features which my partner later confirmed, in astonishment (of course), to be those of his former girlfriend. As the hawk and I stopped on the plateau, the woman turned to us. At that moment, my hawk lifted back into the sky, and I realized that I, too, had become a hawk, and so had the woman: the three of us flew together toward the dawn until, after a time, the young woman peeled off to the left and flew down to darkness. It was clear that she was destined by forces I could not control to be alone for some time.

Nevertheless some part of me, even in this "journey," was incensed. I turned to my guardian angel, the hawk, in fury. "Do you expect me," I asked him, "to go back to this man in San Francisco and tell him that his girlfriend turned into a hawk and flew away from us? Do you expect that to be *healing*? Give me a break. We're all going back to the plateau and start again from there." The hawk looked at me with hawk-like eyes and wheeled back, and suddenly we were back on the plateau—the hawk, the woman (as a woman) and I (as me). To say that this was all very strange would be something of an understatement.

At once we began to sink down into a kind of valley where there were people and houses, rather like Polk Street or Noe Valley in San Francisco, and the man to whom I was to offer a healing vision joined us, and he and the girl did various things that two lovers might do, and I saw them and heard them...but they were also quite specific rather than generic. They entered a kind of dance, intensely erotic, and as the eros waned it was clear that the woman had only been partly there all the time, though the man had been wholly there, and there was something lost about her that he could not fulfill, and he might well die trying: her departure was urgent for her health and for his. All this came out in some detail before the drumming stopped, and as I thanked the hawk for the fuller vision, the lights came up and Harner asked us to report to our partners what we had experienced.

My partner had had no previous shamanic study or experience at all, and thus did not have much to offer by way of insight—as I somehow had guessed; the fate of that woman in my life, I thought, would remain obscure and untraceable for a long time, perhaps forever, a sadness too great to resolve. But as I began to speak to him about what I had seen and what it seemed to me to mean, he sat in perfect stillness and with such as stare as I have only seen in extraordinary moments of teaching. When I was done, he was quiet. "So much of that is true," he said. "It's about things that actually happened. Things you couldn't have known about." Right there, just for a few minutes, I remembered what it might have been like to be a Christian Science practitioner, to have the presence of spiritual blessedness in my soul and the souls of others I might help...but this was a practice seemingly as far from Christian Science as a westerner might imagine. Yet this man who had been my partner was clearly comforted, and had found out from my vision something that he had not understood about why this relationship had to end, and seemed—I use the world carefully—healed.

I left the workshop that afternoon in a kind of rapture: though the weather earlier had been unsettled, a rich sunset spread over the Richmond and Sunset districts of the city, and though it looked like a cliché I didn't care. I drove out to Ocean Beach, walking the sand for an hour at dinnertime as people came out to play, to walk their dogs, to fly kites: it seemed very lovely, suddenly, to be alive, to be human.

Then I drove down into my past, down the Great Highway to Princeton Harbor and the Shore Bird Restaurant, where my mother and father sometimes went for dinner in the 1970's and where I sometimes took dates in those same years. The restaurant was still there, though it had suffered some with the passage of time, and as I ate there, alone, I tried to recall the spirits of all the lost people in my life and tried to imagine them in this place of refuge, this place in the past that still was present and different and the same. And then, in the gathering darkness, I drove farther south, past Half Moon Bay to Pescadero Beach and the sand and ocean I had come to for solace since high school. Standing there, I felt thankful, and only then returned to my strange motel in San Francisco. My eagerness for Harner's teaching and the workshop the next day was fierce.

That night, just after midnight, I awoke to insistent whispering on the second-floor landing outside my slightly-open motel window. At first I thought it was some late guest fumbling for his keys; then I thought, with annoyance, that it must be a drug deal; then I really began to listen. "How would you like me to fuck you, you little cunt," the man was saying. "How would you like my sweet cum in your mouth? Wouldn't you like that, you little prick? Oh yes, yes, oh *yes*..." And I thought: it's a rape—someone is going to be assaulted right outside my window—I need the phone—and then I realized that the phone was on the other side of the room, nowhere near the bed, and that I had to pass in front of the plate glass window of my motel to reach it. But I was about to get up and call 911 when I heard other words: "Oh yeah," the man was saying, "yeah, you, you little cunt, you there in room 53, I've been watching you for three hours now, I've been waiting for you. I'm going to fuck you blind." And at that moment, as this man began to pull at the edge of my window, trying to rip it open, I realized I was the target—I was room 53—this man had been watching me, my body, through a crack in the curtains as I took off my clothes and got in and out of the shower and climbed into bed and read and, finally, turned off the light—and if I didn't get to the phone before he got through the window, my body would no longer be mine, possibly forever.

The phone was unlighted; I flipped on the light; the man saw me, smiled, as he worked harder on the window. I dialed 911; nothing happened; the phone was not wired for 911; everything had to go through the switchboard. In desperation I dialed "O"; after too many rings, a sleepy man answered. "There's a man trying to break through my window," I said, "and I need security *now*." That was the blessing: this man, who turned out to be a combination night clerk and security guard, was on my landing within a minute, and as the rapist heard him he broke off his attack, the guard following him as he ran off. I shivered in a terrible rage and fearfulness: this was what it was like. This was what happened to too many women, to a few men, to too many men. I felt a tremendous nausea.

A few minutes later, having recovered myself somewhat, I dialed "O" again to find out what had happened; the phone rang and rang; no one answered. In horror I realized that, if for any reason this man had not been at the desk earlier, when I had first called, there would have been no one to help. I would have been trapped. The disgust and confusion were too much. What good would it do to try to call the police now—even if I could reach them, even if I could look up the non-911 line and hope someone answered at 12:30 A.M.—since I had neither a perpetrator nor, since the security guard was still gone, a witness? I closed and locked my window, though the uncontrollable room thermostat quickly sent the temperature up to 90 degrees. I took a sleeping pill; I hoped for dawn.

I could not concentrate at the workshop the next morning. The people seemed even odder than the day before, and the gains of that day themselves seemed hollow. The woman I'd met the day before seemed glad to see me, but I was off-balance, without ease. During a question-and-answer session with Harner around noon, I finally said, "Yesterday felt like a great blessing to me. But I'm from out of town, and last night at my motel a man tried to break into my room and rape me. And so I'm wondering—" I stumbled as there were some audible gasps—"I'm wondering whether what you're teaching us here can also protect us. Will this shamanic practice make *us* safer in this world?" Oh yes, Michael Harner said, "Oh yes, it will": but it was too late. I still, I *still* did not know how to deal with danger and trauma, especially when they came in such proximity to the possibility of healing, as they had in childhood. That morning Harner had us end with a journey to the Upper World, the world of our teachers, where we ourselves were to ask for a healing (I wondered if this might have been in response to my question). When I went to my version of this Upper World, and a person appeared who indeed seemed like a teacher, I raged at him: "How could you have left me so defenseless last night?" I cried. "And all the years before—the years of my childhood—when I was sick from things Christian Science didn't cure—how could you have left me?" The man looked profoundly sad; then, in a strange turn of events, the hawk from the Lower World appeared in this same place, and the two of them, I thought, registered a sadness like mourning. But it did not make me feel any better.

When the drumming stopped and the lights came on, I gathered up my notebook and bandana and small bag of things, wove my way quickly through the crowd of bodies coming back into ordinary consciousness, and slammed open the auditorium door. I did not have a comfortable vision, I did not have companionship, I did not even have a way of contacting the one person—the woman I'd met—who had registered some kind of personal hope. Angrily striding to the parking lot, throwing my stuff into the back seat of the rental car, I drove immediately from San Francisco to Cowell College at the University of California, Santa Cruz, which I had wanted to attend as an undergraduate instead of Stanford so many years ago, and spent the afternoon reading quietly in the private library of the college, trying to regain something like equilibrium. Later I called a friend in Palo Alto, where I stayed that night. The next morning I was on a plane back to Iowa; I was gone.

III

Some people simply own too many stories of trauma; they themselves become liabilities, the kind of people one wants to avoid on the street or in the hallway. And Cathy Caruth is wrong when she argues that telling a story of trauma is a way of authorizing an awakening from the trauma, even if the victim does not fully understand the story. The story is just a story: the trauma, prelinguistic, remains.

But here, now, in a Cessna 172 over the forested plain on the way to the Ruth Glacier and Mt. McKinley, I am in something like my element, beyond trauma: a place of nature, the air, but also a place of forces still in balance, lift and thrust and weight and drag in an equation that keeps me 4,500 feet above sea level. It is not that I fear the ground—although it is right, I think, to weigh the measure of its seasons here—but rather that I can say that I belong here, too: the sky can be, temporarily, a kind of home, and though it has its liabilities it also has a release and a comfort quite different from what one finds on the ground—almost as if one were a hawk, as if one were the spirit animal. Almost.

One forgets, more than once, the beauty of Alaska, the danger and the beauty. As I approached Mt. McKinley, its peak above a broken range of clouds that I myself was below, I remembered certain vignettes—the place where the teacher in the Upper World shamanic meditation appeared, a place much like McKinley—and I remembered how, in the face of renewed confusion and despair, I knew the power of that place, even as I raged against all that was ugly and futile and destructive. Now I had brought myself back to such a place in my body, in the body of this airplane, a body not like mine but linked here on pain of death with my body, a mechanical symbiosis to which I had assented. It was enough.

Nearing the glacier, I began to climb: 5,500 feet, 6,500 feet...the glacier sloped slowly upward, its ice like sculpture from the air, with blue glacial ponds like handprints from some deity for whom touching sculpture was permitted. Mountains surrounded me: ahead and slightly to my left, Mt. Hunter at 14,573 feet; Mt. Huntington at 12, 240 feet; Mt. Dickey at 9,845 feet. Behind them were clouds, though the fierce sunlight in the thin air made them seem luminous themselves, and behind and above them was Denali itself, Mt. McKinley, whose peak I could now see. It was vertiginous: for a moment, I felt myself swept up another 12,000 feet to fly at the top of the tallest mountain on the continent. There was a rush into light and the clear sky and the top of the earth; a second later, at 8,500 feet in my Cessna 172, I did a bushplane turn known as a "wingover" and reversed my course at the entrance to the Great Gorge. It was time to go back.

As I turned, flipping the plane in an aileron roll almost 90 degrees sideways before kicking the rudder to flip the back end of the plane around, the cabin flooded with light: I felt as I had felt in the best of my shamanic experiments, when something was not simply with me but at once in and around me, supporting me and leading me on. How could I argue with someone who might say, "That is dangerous illusion?" For here, too, the light as a sensation was irrelevant to my ability to control the airplane, and if I succumbed to the beauty of the light I would crash and die. The danger was real. I did not want to die here. "Who are you, and what do you love?" "I am the light, which I love..." No, it sounds wrong, inhuman. But the light was a comfort, nevertheless, and I stopped thinking for awhile, at least in language, and flew down the Ruth Glacier in a tunnel of light, and had no words for it.

Perhaps Alaska was not to be my home range, at least not in a literal sense. But later, as I flew south of Talkeetna and my words came back to me, I thought: we cannot leave the world behind, but we can re-enter it in such a way that certain voices fall silent, and two other senses remain: the sense of being in one's rightful place, and the sense of a larger rightness that surpasses language.

In everything I had attempted over the past decade, from religion to work to love to shamanism, there had always been some accumulated or acute disaster, some dark counter to the hope I tried to hold. But here, at least, that darkness had lifted in the intense light of the Ruth Glacier, and I felt that certain things were true: the comfort of something like a divine presence or what Tantric Buddhists call our "indestructible drop"; the truth of what I had seen on behalf of my partner at the shamanic workshop; the truth of such journeys, and their fragility; the darkness of the world; the sudden release into love, into wordlessness, into hope.

Perhaps for humans the "home range" was multiple and various, and might come with hard tilling of the soil in a single place or with explorations across the world; it might come with secrecy or resounding knownness; it might come as a spirit as much as a place. Perhaps I had thought of it too narrowly. If there was a place where I might know others and have them know me, if there was a place I could learn to love, and times when language subsided and the truth of certain feeling took over, I could end my commute from the world of spirit to the world of matter; I could cease to be a ghost man. Or so I thought in the air, in Alaska. That was when some of the oldest words I knew came back to me, words that N.

Scott Momaday had taught me decades before from the Navajo Nightway ceremony, a ceremony of restoration and healing. "Restore my feet for me," I said to the Alaskan air, "restore my legs for me, restore my body for me, restore my mind for me, restore my voice for me."

Ahead in the distance was the Anchorage basin, the nexus of humans and their ghosts. "May it be beautiful before me," I said to the Alaskan air. "May it be beautiful behind me, may it be beautiful above me, may it be beautiful below me, may it be beautiful all around me." The radio began to hum with voices; I would be landing soon. "In beauty it is finished," I said to all my ghosts, to my lovers, to my teachers, to my children, to Scott, to all the unbelievers, even me. "In beauty, it is finished." And I went down again, to greet the terrible, beautiful earth.

IV

Detritus and icons:
On the old redwood table at my campsite in a modestly remote part of the California coast, previous tenants have left four things. One is a woman's black headband, darkened to luminousness and disintegration by rain. It sits at a far corner of the table. In the center of the table are three small stones. One is creamy tan, worn smooth to a triangle that approximates the shape of the Point Reyes peninsula, which is where I am. The other two are much rougher. They look a little like small mountain ranges of pale green porcelain, dulled here and there by time and wear. In the center of one of these stones is what looks like a diamond—a crystalline structure, like a lighthouse, or something else immediately metaphorical. Not being an expert, I cannot swear to the identity of these stones, but I would suspect that the first is sandstone, a marine sediment that overlies the granite rocks of the Pacific plate beneath me. The other two, I think, are forms of chert—"rock" composed of the remains of single-celled organisms, like diatoms, and other marine shell material. Daniel Mathews, author of *The Cascade-Olympic Natural History* (not, strictly speaking, relevant here, but such a wonderful guide book that I almost always carry it), writes, "Calcite shells are most familiar to us, but there is also a large group of one-celled organisms that make a sort of shell out of silica, and these are the main sources of chert."

On a bookshelf at my home in Iowa, 2,000 miles away, is a piece of chert I received years ago now from the woman with whom I first plotted my trip to Alaska. Some days it seems like practically the only thing I still have of her, but if that is true it is not a poor gift. Chert has a magical property in its intrinsic variances: from one angle it can appear hard, dull, and stony, while from another it can appear translucent and almost weightless. It is one of the few perfect paradoxes in nature, a thing which says that, by virtue of minerals and of light, it is sometimes a thing and sometimes not—sometimes immanent, sometimes transcendent. But, of course, one needs a human mind to make any sense of this—if it does make sense. What is most remarkable about the one piece of chert on my table is the piece of rock crystal embedded in the center. It glows, in this early afternoon sun, like a small sun itself. Not a poor trapped thing, I think; a slight shift in mineral substance makes all that is solid melt into light.

There is no one else here. It is a weekday in mid-May; on the backcountry permit roster at the Park headquarters, my name was one of only two listed, and the other person (or people accompanying him) haven't shown up yet. The manzanita and coyote brush of my campsite grow above my head, filling the air around me with a fragrance I remember from my teenage years in California—a fragrance of the sun, of warm skin and warm earth, of cool plants, of warm, smooth grass.

After taking off my backpack and setting up my tent, I begin to remove my clothes. First my shoes, socks, pants, underwear; then my shirt. I stand naked by the table, the sun pouring over my skin as it has not done in years, as it has not done, in fact, since I left Alaska. An intense sexual happiness comes over me. There is no one here! Only me, and the trees, the plants, and the California earth. I lie down in the grass on the low hill beside my tent and feel, through my shoulders and back and butt and balls and thighs and calves and ankles and feet, the hard sweetness of the earth, the layer of grass like a blanket. Caressing myself, I imagine a lover, but she brightens into the intensity of the land around me. When I come, it is in an ecstasy of this place.

No rush, nowhere to go or be, no one else to be, only myself, at rest in this beautiful grass. "Who are you, and what do you love?" In this moment I am a happy person conscious of his happiness, and I love the place that makes me happy. I rub the semen on my stomach, letting it dry; it smells electrically clean and fresh. No need to dress; no one to see me or not to see me. No one threatening, no potential rapist, no assailant. No one to judge my imperfect body, my life-long, bone-jutting skinniness, the concavity in my chest for which there is a technical name, my curved spine—so many things that Christian Science never healed, despite my mother's calls to practitioners! Yet I am a beautiful animal here, a healthy animal. This is my place, my *querencia*.

It was Alaska, with all of its hope, both fulfilled and unfulfilled, that reminded me to return here. This is my home. Virtually a wilderness 40 miles north of San Francisco, the Point Reyes peninsula includes 72,000 acres of mountain and shoreline and grassland and high meadow protected by National Park decree. It's relatively untamed, seductive, and private: on a weekday in any season but summer, one can walk the trails for miles without seeing another soul. It resists, has always resisted, my best intentions. I thus come here when I know my intentions need resisting.

Ghost Man

When my body feels warm all the way through for the first time in three years, I go back to the table. Sitting at the table naked is not like sitting there clothed; the bones of my bony buttocks rest uneasily on the hard redwood, and I sense a certain inferiority or embarrassment. One does not come to a table naked. That is a social rule. Even here, virtually in the middle of nowhere, I am intimidated by a table, or rather by the common rules surrounding tables. But here, at least, I can recover an old defense mechanism—I can laugh. The insistent, cool wind above the manzanita takes my laugh away almost before it leaves my mouth. A red-tailed hawk circles above, drops down into the brush 50 yards up the hill from me, flies up, circles again—the behavior not like hunting, more like nesting; but where, in this brush? It seems unlikely; we watch each other, animal and animal. Her talons make me feel small, but not afraid.

Turning back to the four objects on the table, I hold each of them in turn. Who was the woman? The headband is of medium size, a plain plastic band covered in black, unraveling cloth—not garish or excessive, but not small or delicate either. This was not for minor effect; it was to hold hair in place. How did she come to lose it, or leave it? What distracted her? Was she happy here? There are no hairs still attached to the band; has it been here, then, a long time? Or did she shake it off, toss it aside, much as I have tossed everything I wear aside here, in the loveliness of a happy body, and never pick it up again—so that, with days of rain and wind tearing at it, tearing at the remnants of her hair, pulling them all away, it was as if it had never been hers? I lust after the possibilities, more because this is a good place for lust than because I might really learn anything. For the moment, the joys of speculation are better than knowledge.

I'm astonished at how sensual the sandstone feels when I pick it up to rub it between my fingers. There is a softness to this stone I cannot remember feeling with any other rock; it is, as whoever placed it here obviously realized, a remarkable stone. Perhaps because of its softness, perhaps because of the way it curves around like a landform, like a reclining body, I find it womanly, and am taken with its eros. And even though I know that I am beginning to irritate myself—that I now recall being deeply irritated, for example, by the moments in such a celebrated book as Terry Tempest Williams' *Refuge*, in which she applauds the land because it is female, with shapes like "breasts and buttocks," even as she reserves masculine traits for sculptures and other "phallic" impositions on the land, thus politicizing the land itself in a foolish way—I feel *this* stone to be different from the two next to it, and I love the feel and presence of this stone, and see it as *not* "like me," but present with me, like the love of a woman that I myself impute to it, and this comforts me.

As I stare into the crystal in the center of the chert, I do see it as "like me," do respond to the uncountable rough edges and jagged lines, regret them, even though they are beautiful, and look instead to the beauty of jaggedness turned to light. This is what arises from the earth. And these are the emotions they draw forth from me, as I reflect on what it means to be a body—knowing that, by this act of reflection, I am changing the creation in some slight way, am no longer in quite the same creation as the red-tailed hawk a few yards away from me. Sitting perfectly still, I hunt: but she must move to hunt. "Mind is an aspect of matter after all," says Colin McGinn in *The Mysterious Flame*, "but an aspect that does not fit the usual conception of matter." It is an important—though, in the end, perhaps not an essential—difference.

V

At roughly the same time the Chugach terrane was slamming onto the North American continent some 2,500 miles north of here, creating the Chugach Mountains, where I first camped in Alaska, a body of land on the Pacific plate was beginning to move northward and rise out of the ocean, negotiating a tense bond with the North American plate on which most of the United States resides. This land mass, which began in the region of what is now Los Angeles, was Point Reyes. As it moved up along the San Andreas fault, it defined a vast range of geologic difference: granitic landforms atop Mount Wittenberg, for example, quite unlike the Franciscan sandstones east of the fault, indicate both the violent origins of this land and the foreignness of its source.

Point Reyes is barely attached to North America, though it looks secure enough on any map (except a geologic one), and its life here is evidence of the ceaseless motion of the body of this planet—the burning, unconscious destiny to be other than what it now is. This land still moves northward at the rate of about two inches per year; when a major earthquake finally hits the northern San Andreas, it may move a great deal more. Interestingly, only four earthquakes, all ranging from two to three on the Richter scale, hit the Point Reyes area between 1972 and 1989, the year of the big quake along the nearby Hayward Fault that rocked the San Francisco Bay area. A few years are meaningless in relation to geologic time, but they are meaningful to humans, and as one watches and waits for that inevitable upheaval, it is hard to overlook the constant, smaller upheavals that go on underneath Point Reyes.

Though the scale of time here, so obviously similar to that of Alaska, dwarfs human time, and thus tempts one to imagine, as I once did, a life out of time, I have something here that I did not have in Alaska—a long story—and this binds me to the land here in quite a different way. It may be that land, not being "conscious" as we know consciousness, is always indifferent to people, but some places are sacred to some people. This means, in part, that these people "conceive an idea of themselves" (as N. Scott Momaday says) in relation to this sacred place, and this idea of themselves is more powerful there than anywhere else.

To anyone for whom land is a commodity, this idea probably makes no sense. But to those of us who have felt lost or deeply uncertain on this planet, a holy place is where some of the uncertainty vanishes, or where, despite one's various miseries, one feels an underlying reciprocity between land, time, and self. To come to the end of one's human time in a sacred place is not necessarily a tragedy, for one is as at home on this planet as one will ever be. If, after my death, my ashes were scattered in one of the high meadows of Point Reyes—or in the waves of the Mendocino Headlands, another sacred place 100 miles north—I would consider myself to have come home, and would not assume that the reciprocity between the land and me had ended simply because I had died. But, again, that is an article of faith—difficult to argue about with anyone who sees the land as fundamentally other or apart from oneself.

I have always had a peculiar sensation of kinship with this land. Kinship, in my experience, often starts out with a sense of wariness and disbelief: in this respect it's much like love. "I can't believe this is happening," one says, stunned by feeling; "I'm not really feeling this way; *why* am I feeling this way?" These questions, on a more muted level, occupied my mind 30 years ago, when I first caught a glimpse of Point Reyes from Highway 1, on which my parents and I were conducting one of our awful but well-meaning family trips.

Tired and nauseated from the winding road, still suspicious of California after my 13 years of childhood in Pennsylvania, I looked at the strange spectacle of a small mountain range between me and the Pacific—an ocean which had, a few miles back, been a mere stone's throw away—and saw that this land had secrets. Because having a handful of secrets was, I thought in those early teenage years, the only thing between me and some species of madness, I found myself looking back at the Inverness ridge as we drove farther north. At the mouth of Tomales Bay, the long, skinny body of water separating Point Reyes from the mainland, I saw the turbulent sea around the tip of the point and felt the San Andreas under me as if I were connected by a wire. All in all, at that time, I was relieved to leave.

But two years later, in April 1974, I was back, driving a carload of friends through a rainstorm to Drakes Beach, thinking (when I wasn't thinking about the rain, or the unreliable gas gauge on my father's 1966 Chevy Malibu station wagon) about Sebastian Vizcaino, who arrived in Drakes Bay on January 6, 1603, the Day of the Three Kings, and felt it appropriate to honor the day by christening the land "Punta de los Reyes." Interestingly, Vizcaino was part of an earlier contingent that had been shipwrecked at Point Reyes when their galleon was destroyed in Drakes Bay during a sudden storm. Vizcaino's captain, Sebastian Rodriguez Cermeno, and the 70 remaining men traveled for several months in a longboat, finally reaching Mexico in January 1596. It seemed important for Vizcaino, after becoming captain of his own vessel, to return to the place of the wreck, and not only because it was an obvious stopping point on a journey up the coast. Any of a number of other places would have done equally well, and the memory of the wreck could hardly have stood as evidence of the safety of Drakes Bay. Vizcaino came back because he had to name the place that was, in some way, his *querencia,* his refuge, though it had been a refuge whose waters were troubled by death.

These historical reflections were distractions in another way, because my carload of friends was caravaning with another carload of friends, and their car had run into trouble. Just above Stinson Beach, on Highway 1, it had shredded an alternator belt. A few of us had driven back to Mill Valley to buy a new belt from a gas station (whose owner also let us borrow several box-end wrenches in order to replace the belt—the trust at least some people in California had in each other in 1974!) while the rest of us stayed with the wounded car. After replacing the belt, my friends headed back to Mill Valley to return the wrenches; they promised to catch up with us. So we waited awhile, then drove northward slowly, waiting to see them in our mirror. But they never caught up with us.

It had not occurred to us that they might take a different highway in order to beat us to Drakes Beach. For about six hours we drove up and down Highway 1, making ourselves carsick, stopping to check over the edge of the highway at various points as dusk drew near, calling the California Highway Patrol...but no one had seen them. When, finally, around eight o'clock, we pulled into the Drakes Beach parking lot, not knowing what else to do, we found a large message that the tide was just beginning to wash away—"We were here. Where were you?" The trip had been intended as a birthday party for my girlfriend Lesley; by the time we got home, around eleven P.M., our friends had been back for a couple of hours, and though they tried to make discreet inquiries among our parents about whether we had returned, they succeeded in alarming Lesley's mother, who grounded her instantly. She went to her room in tears. We went back to my parents' house, without Lesley, and had a barbecue at midnight.

It ought to have gone down in our private annals as a catastrophic trip, but there had been no shortage of adventure to it, although there was a subterranean grimness to the barbecue that no one wanted to admit, and although later the Point Reyes peninsula did not, apparently, have the best karma for Lesley and me: a year-and-a-half later, in December 1975, she and I came to Point Reyes to seal our break-up, walking along McClure's Beach, picking up pebbles but not showing them to each other, standing miles apart. Later still, though, I came here with friends from college, and with another girlfriend, Sonja, who sat with me on a bluff above the lighthouse and listened to the mingling sounds of the fog horn and the horn from a ship at sea (the harmony of the two tones, a perfect fourth, seemed a stunning accident); and then, in 1977, recalling my original response to this place, I came here with boots and a pack to hike into the backcountry I had not yet seen. In all of these ways and times, this place became my place, a place of personal risk and sorrow and discovery—a place in which I could lay my body down and feel the ghosts of my other bodies here, and find them not threatening but companionable.

But I am here now because, while my personal history makes this land central to me, I am not central to it—even though, when I am here, I am as essential as any other creature. There is a paradox of perception here, but it is the kind of paradox that implies that all dichotomies must ultimately break down. I am interested in this now because I have come to wonder if such breakdowns have organic links, and that, as the uplift and subduction of the continental crust alters the land which nevertheless seems generally solid to us, a psychological equivalent—no less natural than plate tectonics—alters the geography of human life. For love to have a connection to geologic forces is, for me, a way of understanding both the violence and the inevitability of its passion—and to understand how, despite this, it has its periods of stability. This stability is as beautiful as the other kinds of fierce instability we call romantic passion; it endures even as, far beneath the surface, forces are at work to alter or end it. In love, as in symbolic thought, we begin to bypass the orders of animal creation, returning to a different, more elemental level of creation—even as we appear to exceed it through the act of contemplation. Our origins are not precisely those of the animal kingdom; nor is it true that, in the act of contemplation, we create our own origins. What is made is also what is given, in a way not quite consistent with the rest of species: our home range is as much a subduction and uplift as the place that, for a time, overlies these changes. And love, though primarily a mode of contact between human beings, is not *only* a force between humans. Sometimes it is a force between one human and the earth, or one human and an animal; sometimes it is a force between one human and an "object" that he or she can neither name nor limit.

What moved this piece of land where I now stand is different from what moved the land 10 miles to the east. A fault, evolving from molten rock miles below and kin to subduction zones across the crust of the planet, made this land volatile in a way that caused the word "land" to lose all its usual connotations of peacefulness and durability. This land was not like a person; it was not God; but it was like a god to me, or gods, like Shiva and Parvati, or like Shakti, about which Diana Eck, author of *Encountering God*, writes, "Hindus speak of the divine, surging, mothering energy as Shakti, and the Hindu sense of Shakti has time and again steered me toward a larger understanding of the Holy Spirit. Shakti is the feminine aspect of God...It is not the power of the female in particular. It is *all* divine power and energy, and it is conventionally said to be an attribute of the Goddess."

This land is not male and female, with rounded hills, soft valleys, tall, straight conifers...such symbolism is a parody of sexual power. But to feel, here, a nurturing that begins in the violent tumult of the inner earth and ends in strange varieties of earth and shade, of light and sea and secrecy and sensual happiness, is to feel kinship with powers not conventionally human. It is to feel part of some evolutionary process, even if that evolution is not, strictly speaking, of nature; it is to begin to believe that evolution works in more than one way, according to our perception of it, and that the line separating meditative human beings from other animals is also a line suggesting that the creation evolves differently when meditated on, that consciousness is not finally distinct from evolutionary biology, and that evolutionary biology is not finally distinct from spiritual insight.

VI

Human beings are obsessed with origins and destinies. "Who are we? Where do we come from?...Are we capable, if need be, of fundamental change, or do the dead hands of forgotten ancestors impel us in some direction, indiscriminately for good or ill, beyond our control?" Carl Sagan and Ann Druyan ask these questions in *Shadows of Forgotten Ancestors*, but the questions are dignified more by their ubiquity than by their uniqueness. We want to *know* these things. And we want to know them at different levels of abstraction. We want to know, for no obviously very good reason, when people from Asia came across the Bering land bridge—was it 25,000 years ago? 50,000 years ago?—and what their probable route was into central North America. We want to know the relationship between bipedalism, tool use, and gestural or spoken language in early species of the genus *Homo* a million or two million or even five million years ago. But we also want to know who we are individually. We want to know whether there is such a thing as what we commonly call a soul, and whether—when we feel far from home, abandoned or deeply burdened by forces beyond our control—it is possible to return to that soul as if it were a refuge. Is there something to go back to that will guide us forward? Do we each have a private origin?

Such questions, as Sagan and Druyan imply, exist oddly within the strange cognitive void of evolution. "You started with a chaotic, irregular cloud of gas and dust," they write, "tumbling and contracting in the interstellar night. You ended with an elegant, jewel-like solar system, brightly illuminated, the individual planets neatly spaced out from one another, everything running like clockwork. The planets are nicely separated, you realize, because those that aren't are gone." What doesn't fit is wiped out—bam!—gone. Planets are gone. Whole solar systems are gone. This is so even though "gone" means something different here, on earth, on this planet, from what it means on a planet one million light years away, where we cannot help being utterly in each other's past. Being "gone" is relative, which apparently means that being "here" is also relative—though not for us. We exist in the context of "remorseless and sustained violence, where vastly more worlds were destroyed than preserved,"

Sagan and Druyan write. Jonah says to God, whose influence and existence Sagan and Druyan do not acknowledge, "I am cast out of thy sight; yet will I look again toward thy holy temple."

Ironically, what may be most important in this passage is not Jonah's unshakeable faith—though obviously that is crucial—but rather his use of "I." Despite his terror, Jonah is still an "I," by no means convinced of his worthlessness. He will look toward the "holy temple," a synecdoche for God, and will find there his essential identity, wherever that may carry him. It might be possible to say that, even without a belief in a divine force or a soul, one could look far into the universe and its chemical or physical violence as a way of opening a window on one's own soul—so that one's existential destiny might become clear as well.

Or one could turn away from the heavens, and look at humans alone. Emile Durkheim, in *The Elementary Forms of the Religious Life*, observes that God *is* society, and that, as Tomoko Masuzawa explains it, "the hidden identity of the sacred turns out to be something eminently unifying, namely, social sentiment, or more famously, 'collective effervescence,' which, being the power uniting individuals into a group, designates the essence of society, according to Durkheim." Who needs a private soul when all that is sacred emerges only from human society? If Durkheim is to be trusted, then I should find my origins in the sentiment of the sacred which binds me to other people; that sentiment depends fundamentally on a distinction between sacred and profane. If to search for a private soul is a profanation of the sacred, then I ought to find a way to release myself from this quest, recover a community that is sacred by virtue of its community, and free myself from unanswerable questions.

Later, however, Durkheim writes, "There is nothing...with which to characterize the sacred in relation to the profane except their heterogeneity." It's an extraordinary observation: at any moment the "sacred" and the "profane" are capable of changing places, and even when each is in place as a linguistic and social construct, each interpenetrates the other. Masuzawa, a contemporary cultural theorist, comments, "having observed that the sacred-profane distinction is the universal characteristic of all religions, Durkheim maintains that the sacred itself is without any determinable characteristic; in fact, the only possible determination of the sacred is that it is absolutely heterogeneous with its opposite, the profane."

The use of "heterogeneous" is important, since its Greek roots, *"heter"* and *"genos,"* carry the implication of kinship: the sacred is akin to the profane. This seems itself a profane statement unless one understands—like Durkheim—that it is the evolution of a social idea about the sacred which divides the continuum of sacred and profane. But one could also be more literal about this, claiming that since the sacred and profane are one continuum, one's own version of sacredness would have to include a reconciliation with the profane.

If transformative love, for example—which changes me fundamentally, makes me stronger and happier, and convinces me that I occupy an appropriate place in this universe—is sacred to me, then anything which speaks to the absence of that love ought to be profane. The core, mantle, and crust of the earth appear fully physical and loveless, transforming themselves merely according to chemical dicta; they must be profane. The same could be said for plants, for trees, for thousands of species of animals. What is sacred to me is the lover who shows me who I am, who finds herself equally through me, and who shares with me a sense that what we discover through our love is not deterministic or formulaic but new, regenerative, and conscious of its creativity as if it were a primal creator.

Yet I wonder: if that "other" never comes, or comes repeatedly only to leave, am I then denied access to the sacred? Is my domain, finally, "merely" profane, especially given the matter of heterogeneity? A friend of mine said some years ago, "The difference between you and me is that you have loved and lost, and I have never lost." It was not meant as a statement of superiority—I think—only a statement of fact. Still, the sacred looks different after a transformative love collapses or goes underground. Is it possible, then, to accept the kinship of sacred and profane—to say, for example, "My sources lie in the heart of the profane, in the tectonics of the earth's crust and their chemical compounds, in the way each of these affirms my ability to see, to feel, and to imagine?" A thinker such as Colin McGinn might well reject this, despite his emphasis on consciousness as a deep mystery, because there is simply no demonstrable connection between consciousness itself and matter: our cognitive facilities, he writes, "are not designed to fathom what *links* mind to brain." This is a different issue, however, from the one in which certain kinds of so-called material forces move freely between "profane" and "sacred." Accepting the profane as the sacred, I love the sandstone and the chert on my table at Coast Camp at Point Reyes because they confirm for me something wordlessly real about my own existence.

But this is only partially true. I am also attracted to the stones because someone I do not know chose them from myriad other stones and brought them back here. I love them because a ghost-presence, a human being I will never knowingly meet, saw something beautiful or curious in these stones, and because what he or she and I saw in them is probably remarkably similar. It is not the stones alone that affirm my presence here, but rather the interest and care—the love—of whomever came before me.

If, however, I have been seeking a transformative love all these years, why do I now want so much to be affirmed? What is the difference between transfomative love and affirmative love? It was transformative love that I first knew, or learned about, in my life—love that could lift me out of my morasse of personal sadness and confusion, love that could make me whole, could make me more in the "image and likeness of God." In all these years, it only incidentally occurred to me that what I needed, and rarely received, was affirmative love—love that affirmed my being in this world, exactly and precisely as it was. Point Reyes as a place affirms my present being, my right to be a creature in this world. In the midst of this affirmation I can say that, under certain circumstances, it may be impossible to give one answer to the question, "What do you love," because multiple answers will appear to contradict each other. For years I answered, "I love the idea of being spiritual, or being liberated from my human body"; I also answered, simultaneously though in the psychic version of a whisper, "I love being who I am, and giving and receiving affection." These two answers cancelled each other out, and the result was silence. Interestingly, one would have thought that someone who, deep in his heart, desired the affirmation of human love would have found a way to make that voice stronger by living more fully in the culture of his time; but our entire culture is caught in the contradiction between transformative and affirmative love.

Though, in the end, there may be no story to tell about love, right now a story of love is very much on my mind, and it is a story of confusion. For so long I have sought after, prayed for, and otherwise waited to be transformed—by love, by God. There is not a murmur here, not a whisper, about love that affirms, "I cherish you simply and exactly in these circumstances and terms." But this may be why, for example, the life of Jesus, which I have previously described as a story of failed love, is not a failure after all—rather an indictment of our ways of telling the story. Jesus fails because his love is primarily affirmative, and we seek transformation; when he is transformed after death, we accept that as the essential measure of his life story, and twist all that comes before into a teleology of transcendence. The *point* of it all, in short, is to overcome mortality, to be born again. But no; there is not one point but many, and one of these is to love that which one finds, though it be unloveable, doubtful, or even apparently impervious to love.

When Jesus goes in to Lazarus, he weeps, knowing the unnaturalness of what he must do. He is torn by transformative and affirmative desires. But in the end he does not say, "Lazarus, become the perfect spiritual being you know yourself to be." He says, "Lazarus, come forth." Lazarus, come back into this world; step out among us; be with me. I love you. I love *you*. This affirmation, routinely overlooked in the refulgence of Lazarus' resurrection, *is* love. And, indeed, Lazarus is untransformed, merely—merely!—brought back from the dead to be who he was, which surely is part of his terror. Nevertheless, the immanent love of Jesus is Lazarus' reassurance, and no doubt his *querencia* in that moment when the fabric of the universe itself tears.

Always to seek transformation is to tell oneself stories that have no possible resolution, because ultimately transformation must end in death or silence. The end of transformation is not love, but something more awful or unspeakable.

Thomas Simmons

And the method of transformation is inevitably the method of destruction. Something, or someone, is destroyed to make room for the new; this is the paradigm for religious encounters with the spirit and for romantic relationships as well. But, whereas in the religious encounter, one comes to believe that a version of oneself has died, in the romantic version the casualties may be much greater. Moving from partner to partner, endlessly seeking the transformation no other human may be capable of providing, one leaves a trail of grief and mistrust, as cast-off lovers curse love for the scars they bear.

Romantic love is not love, but a kind of war fought without Pentagon weapons. And, while it is true that mating conventions vary wildly in the evolutionary chain—chimpanzees with many mates, for example, orangutans mating for life, elk or moose locked in combat for the privilege of mating with several females—it is not right to place romantic love anywhere on the evolutionary scale. Its effect is wholly other than what occurs in nature when orangutans choose each other, when several male chimps mate with one female, or even when a male lion eats his own offspring. There may be, strictly speaking, no "damage" in any of these cases; however, when human beings reflect on their own suffering, consume themselves with doubt, and fear that a sustaining love may never find them, they implicitly call the worth—and the survivability—of their species into question. They inhabit a world whose primary trait is its otherworldliness, its alienation from this creation.

Because I have spent too much of my life in this other world, I have begun to tell myself that there must be a way in which affirmative love, rather than transformative love, is more consistent with the nature of *Homo sapiens.* Though this may be a hopeful lie, it is at least an interesting one, since it overturns a prejudice in favor of radical transformation inherent in both Christianity and romanticism. It says, "I will first try to be a creature among creatures; I will come forth first, rather than trying to ascend." But it is a strange thing to say this. For although claiming some kind of affirming love would seem to yield many possible stories, the immediate result for me is silence. My mind goes blank; I look around; there is no one here; I do not know what to say.

An impasse. Time to walk.

Pulling on a bathing suit and a t-shirt, stepping from my campsite through long beach grass to the trail, I walk perhaps a half-mile through meadow and low brush until I come to a beautiful stream, hidden from above by heavy bracken. It curves out to the southern tip of Limantour Beach, and then into the Pacific. There is no way over; the stream is too wide; I wade across, although I cannot see the bottom and quickly regret my decision. Startled at the depth and coldness of the water as it quickly reaches my thighs, I stop for a fraction of a second, turn to retreat, then feel the sharpness of the cold so suddenly that I leap forward, where the bank begins to rise until, a few seconds later, I'm on dry sand on the other side. A typical crossing in nature—beautiful, unfathomable, dangerous...with no turning back. I'm struck for a moment by how readily the world lends itself to interpretation. But the day is brilliantly sunny, a remarkable day even for Point Reyes, and after circling in the sand like a bush plane coming in for a landing, I find a spot I like and fling myself down. I imagine feeling each tiny grain of sand against my back until, losing track of the grains, I fall asleep in the omniscient sun.

VII

When I awake, I do not know where I am. I wake to the brilliant light and sound of surf, to the cliffs above me. The sun is low on the horizon. I am alone, Crusoe. Delighted, I begin to recover myself. But a strange feeling, as if I were on the edge of extinction, remains.

On the Point Reyes peninsula there have been three major extinctions or eradications in the last 300 years. The first was the native American presence here, the Miwok coastal Indians whose population went from approximately 3,000 to 300 between 1776 and 1834, the first two generations of the Spanish settlement. The second and third were bear—both black and grizzly. According to Jules Evens, author of the excellent *Natural History of the Point Reyes Peninsula*, the last grizzly was killed in Tulare County in 1922, with the last sighting in the Point Reyes area in 1884. The most recent sighting of a black bear was in 1972, but that was, as Evens says, "equivocal." "The isolation of Marin's [and Point Reyes'] forests from those of the northern coastal counties by the open grasslands of the Sonoma-Marin borderland are likely to impede recolonization of Point Reyes by this gentler cousin of the grizzly," Evens concludes.

In a moment when time and space seem to ripple like sand in the wind, I see men down the beach pulling fish from the sea, women drying them back at the dunes' edge. When they have enough, they will stop, go back to their settlement among the trees in the higher grasslands a mile east of here, or hunt for other game, or simply walk, or play with their children. Though they do not grow crops—no corn here, no wheat—they know the abundance of this place well. As they need to, they harvest fish, abalone, and seaweed; hunt squirrel, duck, rabbit, deer; make food or medicine from the more than 250 plant species they recognize (including the buckeye, whose poison they must first extract); clothe themselves, protect themselves from the weather, and store supplies, using animal skins, redwood bark (fashioned into small houses called "tule kotchas"), and twined roots—sedge roots, redbud roots—for baskets. A prosperous people, they are within one or two moons of Big Time, when they will gather food, the essentials of shelter, and items for trade—dried fish, abalone shells, baskets, clam disc beads—and journey to another part of what is now Northern California, where they will meet with other prosperous tribes from all over the north.

This vision is so enticing that I find my body shifting involuntarily toward the men and women I see, and thus they vanish—but only *as if* they were never there. In fact, they were here far longer than I or any of my Euro-American predecessors. I wonder sometimes if the land keeps a memory of them, as it does of any species driven away or driven to extinction, so that a man or woman in search of ghosts can, if he or she is careful, find in the land the threads of vision that return the lost ones to life. Certainly the few remaining Miwok, straddling two cultures with increasing success, know that memory, know the ghosts as familiars, companions. And certainly some force in the world must keep a record, if only in a substratum we do not recognize as consciousness, of what has been lost.

A version of the loss, recorded in the dry language of traditional anthropology in a book called *The Natural World of the California Indians*, gives a bare taste of what occurred. "During the mission period," Robert Heizer and Albert Elasser write, "the death toll [of Indians] was exorbitant...While the labor demanded of the Indians in the mission was steady, it does not seem to have been unduly harsh. The Indians, however, were by their old custom unused to steady work all day every day, and when they malingered [sic] they were usually punished with the lash at the order of the priest...The priests, celibate in accord with their vows, did not have an enlightened view of Indian sexual customs. They considered their native charges to be immoral by nature, and thought it their duty to lead them into a moral way of life...For individuals who found the mission life intolerable because of culture shock, the scarcity of food, the death of family members, or punishment for minor infractions, the maximum response was to run away." Heizer and Elsasser's statistics give a wider meaning to the fate of the coastal Miwok: "In the brief span of 65 years of mission operation," they write, "extending from the first founding (1769) to the secularization of the missions (1834), 81,000 Indians were baptized in the missions, and 60,600 deaths were recorded." Over 1,000 recorded deaths a year, in a total native population estimated at 300,000, perhaps half of whom were in contact with the Spanish. Thus, in about 60 years, almost half of those 150,000 were dead, most of the rest were "little better than slaves" (Heizer and Elsasser's words) in the missions, and the rest were dispersed. By 1821, according to the National Park Service, virtually all the Miwok on the Point Reyes peninsula had been taken "to labor in Spanish missions. Except for a few who managed to evade the missionaries, and some survivors of the missions who wandered back after the Mexican revolution, Point Reyes had seen the last of its original inhabitants."

Some theologians hold that God needs us—needs the creation—to be His witness, to establish the reciprocity that confirms His identity, and—most of all—to make it possible for love to exist and to further the creation. Love, in this view, cannot exist within one being, even an omnipotent one. Being relational, love can exist only between two created forms, or God and a created form. I have always had trouble with the idea that God needed anything; here, however, recalling the enslavement of the Miwok, I remember how consciousness can be a witness, and how an act of seeing into the past—if the gaze is humble and self-effacing—may be an act of recovery. To recall the Miwok and their near-destruction is to offer the love of remembrance, if only in a minor key—and with no guarantee that it will be or can be accepted. But it is also to remember what else was lost—a range of human freedom that was emphatically not a sentimental fantasy.

In *In the Absence of the Sacred*, Jerry Mander writes, "Millions of people still alive on this earth never wished to be part of this machine and, in many cases, are not. I am speaking of people who have lived on the fringes of a technological world...These are people whose ancestors and who themselves have said from the beginning of the technological age that our actions and attitudes are fatally flawed, since they are not grounded in a real understanding of how to live on the earth." As someone who grew up "on the fringes of the technological world" at least in one sense—lacking medicine and medical physicians because of my religion—I can say that a society of diminished technology is by no means an asset in itself, and that a child who dies of a treatable illness because her parents prefer prayer to available medicine is a child who has died in a repugnant way. Yet Mander is right to question the "machine" of our lives. It is not, after all, monolithic, although Jean Baudrillard points out in *The Mirror of Production* how thoroughly its language of "value" is wired into our thinking. Rather, the machine is almost infinitely fragmentable. The question for anyone who feels trapped by the machine is, first of all, "Where should I push to break through the fragments?"

Here is a provisional answer, known to the Miwok and, less commonly, to Anglo society: our ghosts return to keep us from becoming ghosts. These ghosts and I share this: we imagine ourselves in contact with a reality that could destroy us but does not. This is the reality of primal power—turbulent, overwhelming, erotic—which manifests itself at times as tectonic (as it does to me here on the point), at other times as something animal—like the bears here, ghost bears as Edward Grumbine would explain, but present still, like the bear in Maxine Kumin's "In the Park":

> You have forty-nine days between
> death and rebirth if you're a Buddhist.
> Even the smallest soul could swim
> the English Channel in that time
> or climb, like a ten-month-old child,
> every step of the Washington Monument
> to travel across, up, down, over, or through
> —you won't know till you get there which to do.

Thomas Simmons

> *He laid on me for a few seconds*
> said Roscoe Black, who lived to tell
> about his skirmish with a grizzly bear
> in Glacier Park. *He laid on me*
> *not doing anything. I could feel*
> *his heart beating against my heart.*
> Never mind *lie* and *lay,* the whole world
> confuses them. For Roscoe Black you might say
> all forty-nine days flew by.
>
> I was raised on the Old Testament.
> In it God talks to Moses, Noah,
> Samuel, and they answer.
> People confer with angels. Certain
> animals converse with humans.
> It's a simple world, full of crossovers.
> Heaven's an airy Somewhere, and God
> has a nasty temper when provoked,
> but if there's a Hell, little is made of it.
> No long-tailed Devil, no eternal fire,
>
> and no choosing what to come back as.
> When the grizzly bear appears, he lies/lays down
> on atheist and zealot. In the pitch-dark
> each of us waits for him in Glacier Park.

From real contact with the real bear come the stories that define us, as Kumin's poem suggests. The bear we wait for may be in Glacier Park, or the Chugach National Forest, or Point Reyes, or—of course—she may be in versions of each of these places within our hearts. We know when we make contact. The bear may be the death of a lover, parent, child; an accident; an assault; a divorce; a terrible depression; one's own imminent death. There is a pause: the bear takes us, or does not. If not, we return like Lazarus. Yet before these stories of transformation comes one primal story, one primal affirmation: the real bear in the real world—deadly, but choosing this time not to kill.

VIII

The ghost man walks over ground he has walked in every human generation. He feels the ground moving northward beneath his feet; a scientist would calculate the rate as .00022 miles per hour, approximately. He is not a scientist.

The breath of animals crosses his path, and he knows them: rabbit, red-tailed fox, skunk, coyote, tule elk, bobcat, black bear, grizzly bear. He names the plants as he does each evening to hear their names: manzanita, columbine, coastal blue larkspur, foxglove, western pennyroyal, selfheal, live-forever. The naming goes on for hours, and then he repeats it, like a poem.

Over time he has been many men, many ghosts, and has died in almost uncountable ways, most of them connected to grief. He has died from sadness at the loss of his home and livelihood; he has died from the grief of lost love; he has died, a suicide, from despair at the impossibility of knowing himself or the world; he has been murdered by invaders, by sadistic interrogators, by soldiers, by business partners, by lovers, by friends, by animals. He has died in the claws of a bear. In the end, which is always now, he is always more than the sum of these deaths. He will be here even if no one comes, even if the land is destroyed by firefight or nuclear winter. When this quadrant of the earth shreds itself millennia from now, he will rise with it, or descend with it, until his being gradually and fully disperses into the magma of his origin. Then something else will occur. But now, this is his place.

It is not necessary for him to have any meaning at all, but since meaning is necessary for humans, and he knows this, he is watchful, and listens to the humans who come here. Some come because they are already kin to him, and know it, although they do not know him. He watches them. It is easy to follow them as they make their way through the grasslands, through the forest trails, or down to the sea; they move so slowly, pause so often. In a moment he could be wherever it would take them hours to go. But they need him, because they are still enmeshed in chaos. They pursue the lovers who will spurn them, they destroy themselves with vain hopes, they waste years of training and stability on one passion which cannot possibly succeed. He knows them.

At night, in their sleep, he comes to them. He shows each something different. Some see a fire burning across a prairie; some see, in the midst of despair, the lover to whom they may yet be faithful, who will finally be faithful to them; some see a direction, a future. Some see only the universe as he sees it: Cassiopeia, Andromeda, Taurus, Orion, Pegasus—and the two bears, Ursa minor and Ursa major, the big dipper, one arm pointing north. For these dreamers he cannot create meaning. He can give only the vision.

This group is always troublesome, unpredictable. Some take up astrology; others return to physics, astrophysics, or fine art; some travel in the direction of the first star they see. Some forget their waking, only to remember it later in moments of great sorrow, which they repeat incessantly—another love which has not saved them, leaving them again. He remains with all of these, unable to alter their responses, but knowing that what they see is what they must see. Eventually they will become like him. They will always be more than the sum of their deaths.

XIX

At night, I awake suddenly in the total, clear darkness. Through the netting on my tent I see the Big Dipper directly overhead, brighter than I have ever seen it before. Sighting off the dipper, I find the north star. It could be a sign to me, or not; it could simply be the night sky. In the same way, this book could have a conclusion almost as an omen, or it could have simply these words: I live in an equilibrium that is constantly on fire, and so do you. We tell ourselves tales of order against the day of our immolation. Some of us burn, or contract under massive pressure, over and over again, to become the mineral or crystal we most cherish in a region of ourselves we cannot name. We, too, have destinies, like the earth's. Others of us live stable lives, riding atop a great fire on a smooth trip through love and family and career. What links us underneath is the fire of the mantle, the burning hem of the garment that heals, and kills, and heals.

I wanted to write a love story, or a story about love, in which difficult questions would have difficult, but ultimately rewarding, answers. But love is a ghost, not subject to dichotomies or categories, now affirmative, now transformative, now healing, now punishing, now refining and clarifying, now troubling and darkening...and always there is nothing there. In the Upanishads, Uddalaka speaks to his son:

"Bring me a fig."

"Here it is, father."

"Break it open. What do you see inside?"

"Some rather tiny seeds, father."

"Break one of them open. What do you see inside?"

"Nothing at all, father."

"From the inside of this tiny seed, which seems to be nothing at all, this whole fig tree grows. That is the Real. That is the *atman*. That art thou, my son."

Out of nothing, out of an inarticulate hopefulness and enflamed desire, my sons and daughter were born; they wait, now, for my return. I care for them, and am present with them, far more than my father cared for or was present with me, and yet I remember my own father largely as a good father—a failure only in the sense that he did not live more of his life, that he shoved that life aside to be "a good father." It is sad what he lost. There is no quantity on earth greater than the quantity of human loss and sadness—unless it is the nothingness out of which love springs, that flame, dwarf star, that Real.

I stare at Ursa major. I have paid too little attention to the land on which I rest, having lived so greatly in my own head these past few days. But I began here as a happy body, and now, staring at this sure clue to the north star, I remember that I am a body called to migration. I am a creature. My brain, I know from recent cognitive research, cannot make rational decisions without its emotional faculties. As Antonio Damasio writes in *Descartes' Error*, my brain is crippled without the emotions. It is not a set of boxed organisms or counting-houses, linked by the synaptic equivalent of wires, but a set of intricately interwoven systems, sacred and profane. I have a remarkable ability to define the borders myself. What is "brain," and what is "perceived"? Who is the "self," and who is the "other"? Jessica Benjamin writes, "The capacity to enter into states in which distinctness and union are reconciled underlies the most intense experience of adult erotic life." To be oneself, and oneself with the other, is to live in eros, at the heart of the world. But the heart of the world itself is never one thing to be defined. To point to an end, a final meaning, is always to point to nothing.

That should be—has been, in my past—a terrifying thought. But now, in the middle of this clear night, I lie awake beneath stars that remind me of the inaccessibility of every origin and the improvisation of every destiny. An improviser by nature, I still look toward the holy temple. Eons cross the night sky, measured in magnitudes of light from the most distant visible star. The earth shifts slightly beneath my body. Between Castor and Pollux, low on the western horizon, I see a configuration I do not recognize, and before it fades I know it to be the ghost man, my kin in the night sky, my *querencia*, my nothingness, my self, your self, love.

Thomas Simmons

Notes

(The notes below refer primarily to authors or works cited incompletely or mentioned in passing in the text itself.)

Pages 20: Robert Pinsky, "The Garden," *History of My Heart* (New York: Ecco, 1984), p. 45.

Pages 29-30: Joseph de Maistre, quoted in Isaiah Berlin, *The Crooked Timber of Humanity* (New York: Knopf, 1991), p. 111.

Pages 34-35: A useful scholarly corollary to these reflections is Jacques Vauclair's *Animal Cognition: An Introduction to Modern Comparative Psychology* (Cambridge, Mass.: Harvard University Press, 1996). Among many authoritative studies at once empirical and anecdotal, see Frans de Waal's *Good Natured: The Origins of Right and Wrong in Humans and Other Animals* (Cambridge, Mass.: Harvard University Press, 1996), and, more recently, *The Ape and the Sushi Master: Cultural Reflections of a Primatologist* (New York: Basic Books, 2001). Questions of comparative cognitive ability and animal identity underlie Kathleen Gibson's and Tim Ingold's anthology *Tools, Language, and Cognition in Human Evolution* (Cambridge: Cambridge University Press, 1993) and Tim Ingold's anthology *What Is an Animal?* (London: Routledge, 1988). Similar questions merit the central focus of Donald R. Griffin's *Animal Minds* (Chicago: Chicago University Press, 1992), though the definitions of conscious behavior in that book seem oddly unproblematic.

Page 40: Frank and John Craighead's research cited in R. Edward Grumbine, *Ghost Bears* (Washington, D.C. /Covelo, Calif.: Island Press, 1992), p. 57; Jon Almack's home range estimate cited in Grumbine, p. 75.

Pages 40-41: See Thomas McNamee, *The Grizzly Bear* (New York: Penguin, 1990), p. 58; Arnie Dood's research cited in Grumbine, p. 76; wolf dispersion discussed in Rick Bass, *The Ninemile Wolves* (New York: Ballantine, 1993), p. 13.

Page 60: See the U. S. Bureau of the Census, *Statistical Abstract of the United States*, 117th ed. (Washington, D. C.: Government Printing Office, 1997); also the National Safety Council, *Accident Facts 1998* (Itasca, Illinois, 1998), p. 121.

Page 62: Kenneth Fields, "Trout Watching," *Smoke* (Duluth, Minnesota: Knife River Press, 1975), unnumbered pages.

Page 63: N. Scott Momaday, *The Way to Rainy Mountain* (Albuquerque: University of New Mexico Press, 1969), p. 8.

Page 64: Ake Hultkrantz, *The Religions of the American Indians* (Berkeley: University of California Press, 1979), p. 73. For a further perspective on the work of Hultkrantz, see Alice Kehoe, "Eliade and Hultkrantz: The European Primitivism Tradition," *American Indian Quarterly,* 20 (Summer/Fall 1996), pp. 377-392.

Page 64: Irvin Howe quoted in Charles L. Woodard, *Ancestral Voice: Conversations with N. Scott Momaday* (Omaha: University of Nebraska Press, 1989), p. 141.

Page 65: Andy Russell quoted in John McPhee, *Coming into the Country* (New York: Bantam, 1978), p. 64.

Page 71-73: John Bierhorst, *The Mythology of North America* (New York: William Morrow, 1985); Gary Snyder, *The Practice of the Wild* (Berkeley: North Point Press, 1990), pp. 155-169; Grumbine, pp. 69-71; Catherine McClellan, *The Girl Who Married the Bear: A Masterpiece of Indian Oral Tradition* (Ottawa: National Museums of Canada, 1970).

Page 72: Maria Johns quoted in Snyder, p. 164.

Page 75: Diane Middlebrook, "To You, Seated Near a Lamp," *Sequoia: Twentieth Anniversary Issue, Poetry 1956-1976*, ed. Michael J. Smith and Dana Gioia (Stanford, 1976), p. 53.

Page 78: A. Young, "The Dimensions of Medical Rationality: A Problematic for the Psychosocial Study of Medicine," quoted in Tamar Kaplan, "An Intercultural Communication Gap: North American Indian vs. the Mainstream Medical Profession," *Doctor-Patient Interaction*, ed. Walburga von Raffler-Engel (Amsterdam/Philadelphia: John Benjamins Publishing Co., 1989), pp. 45-59.

Page 85: See Daniel Dennett, *Darwin's Dangerous Idea: Evolution and the Meanings of Life* (New York: Simon and Schuster, 1995), p. 370.

Page 86: Wendell Berry, "To the Unseeable Animal," *Collected Poems* (Berkeley: North Point Press, 1984), pp. 140-141.

Page 88: See Antonio Damasio, *Descartes' Error: Emotion, Reason, and the Human Brain* (New York: Grosset/Putnam, 1994), p. 243; the more recent *The Feeling of What Matters: Body and Emotions in the Making of Consciousness* (New York: Harcourt, 1999) extends this theory; and see Steven Pinker, *The Language Instinct* (New York: HarperPerennial, 1995), pp. 81-82.

Page 89: Michael C. Corballis, "On the Evolution of Language and Generativity," *Cognition,* 44 (1992), 197-226; Dennett, p. 376.

Page 90: David F. Armstrong, William C. Stokoe, and Sherman E. Wilcox, *Gesture and the Nature of Language* (Cambridge: Cambridge University Press, 1995), pp. 52, 57-63.

Pages 90-91: In addition to the work by Johanson, Johanson, and Edgar listed below, see Donald Johanson and Maitland A. Edey, *Lucy: The Beginnings of Humankind* (New York: William Morrow, 1981); Donald Johanson and James Shreeve, *Lucy's Child: The Discovery of a Human Ancestor* (New

York: William Morrow, 1989); and, most recently, Yohannes Haile-Selassie's discoveries as reported in the *New York Times*, 12 July 2001, p. A12, and more fully in *Nature*, 412: 6843 (12 July 2001).

Page 91-92: Dale Peterson and Jane Goodall, *Visions of Caliban: On Chimpanzees and People* (Boston: Houghton Mifflin, 1993), pps. 33, 34.

Pages 92-93: Donald Johanson, Lenora Johanson, and Blake Edgar, *Ancestors: In Search of Human Origins* (New York: Villard Books, 1994), pp. 78, 81; Harrow Harlow's "technology of love" is described in Donna Haraway, *Primate Visions: Gender, Race, and Nature in the World of Modern Science* (New York: Routledge, 1989), pp. 231-243.

Page 93: Carol Gilligan, "Remapping the Moral Domain: New Images of Self in Relationship," in *Mapping the Moral Domain*, ed. Carol Gilligan et. al. (Cambridge: Harvard University Graduate School of Education, 1989), pp. 8-9.

Page 94: A. N. Wilson, *Jesus: A Life* (New York: Fawcett Columbine, 1992), p. 168.

Page 95: Noel W. Smith, "Brain, Behavior, and Evolution," *The Psychological Record*, 32 (1982), pp. 483-490.

Page 98: Geza Vermes, *Jesus the Jew: A Historian's Reading of the Gospels* (Philadelphia: Fortress Press, 1973), p. 79.

Page 107: Stephen Dobyns, "Querencia," *Cemetery Nights: Poems by Stephen Dobyns* (New York: Penguin, 1987), pp. 94-97.

Pages 109-111: See Kehoe, *American Indian Quarterly*, 20 (Summer/Fall 1996), esp. pp. 377-378; Olga Kharitidi, *Entering the Circle: A Russian Psychiatrist's Journey into Siberian Shamanism* (Albuquerque: Gloria Publishing, 1995); Michael Harner, *The Way of the Shaman* (San Francisco: Harper San Francisco, 10th Anniversary Edition, 1990); Harold Bloom, *Omens of Millennium: The Gnosis of Angels, Dreams, and Resurrection* (New York: Riverhead Books, 1996); Cathy Caruth, *Unclaimed Experience: Trauma, Narrative, and History* (Baltimore: Johns Hopkins University Press, 1996).

Page 120: Colin McGinn, *The Mysterious Flame: Conscious Minds in a Material World* (New York: Basic Books, 1999), esp. pp. 139-174.

Page 123: Diana Eck, *Encountering God: A Spiritual Journey from Bozeman to Banaras* (Boston: Beacon Press, 1993), p. 136.

Pages 124-125 Carl Sagan and Ann Druyan, *Shadows of Forgotten Ancestors* (New York: Ballantine, 1992), pp. 4, 15.

Page 125: Emile Durkheim, *The Elementary Forms of the Religious Life* (New York: Free Press, 1993), quoted in Tomoko Masuzawa, *In Search of Dreamtime: The Quest for the Origin of Religion* (Chicago: University of Chicago Press, 1993), pp. 35-36.

Page 129: Jules Evens, *The Natural History of the Point Reyes Peninsula* (Point Reyes, Calif.: Point Reyes National Seashore Association, 1993), pp. 150-151.

Pages 130-131: Robert F. Heizer and Albert B. Elsasser, *The Natural World of the California Indians* (Berkeley: University of California Press, 1980), pp. 227-228.

Page 131: Jerry Mander, *In the Absence of the Sacred: The Failure of Technology and the Survival of the Indian Nations* (San Francisco: Sierra Club Books, 1991), p. 191; Jean Baudrillard, *The Mirror of Production*, trans. with intro. by Mark Poster (St. Louis: Telos Press, 1975).

Pages 131-132: Maxine Kumin, "In the Park," *Nurture: Poems* (New York: Penguin, 1989), p. 37.

Page 134: Upanishad quotation from Eck, p. 125.

About the Author

Thomas Simmons, associate professor of English and Nonfiction Writing at the University of Iowa, is the author of three previous books: *The Unseen Shore: Memories of a Christian Science Childhood* (Beacon Press, 1991); *A Season in the Air: One Man's Adventures in Flying* (Ballantine Books, 1993); and *Erotic Reckonings: Mastery and Apprenticeship in the Work of Poets and Lovers* (University of Illinois Press, 1994). Following a Stegner Fellowship in poetry at Stanford University and an internship at the *Christian Science Monitor*, he published poems and essays in the *Atlantic*, the *New Republic*, the *Threepenny Review*, the *New York Times Sunday Magazine*, and numerous other magazines and journals. His essays on poetry in the *Christian Science Monitor* were nominated for a Pulitzer Prize in criticism in 1982. A former instructor in English at Stanford University and UC Berkeley, and a former assistant professor at the Massachusetts Institute of Technology, he now resides in Grinnell, Iowa, where he continues his work as a father, poet, and scholar.

Printed in the United States
2688